50 FAVOURITE HOUSES BY
FRANK LLOYD WRIGHT

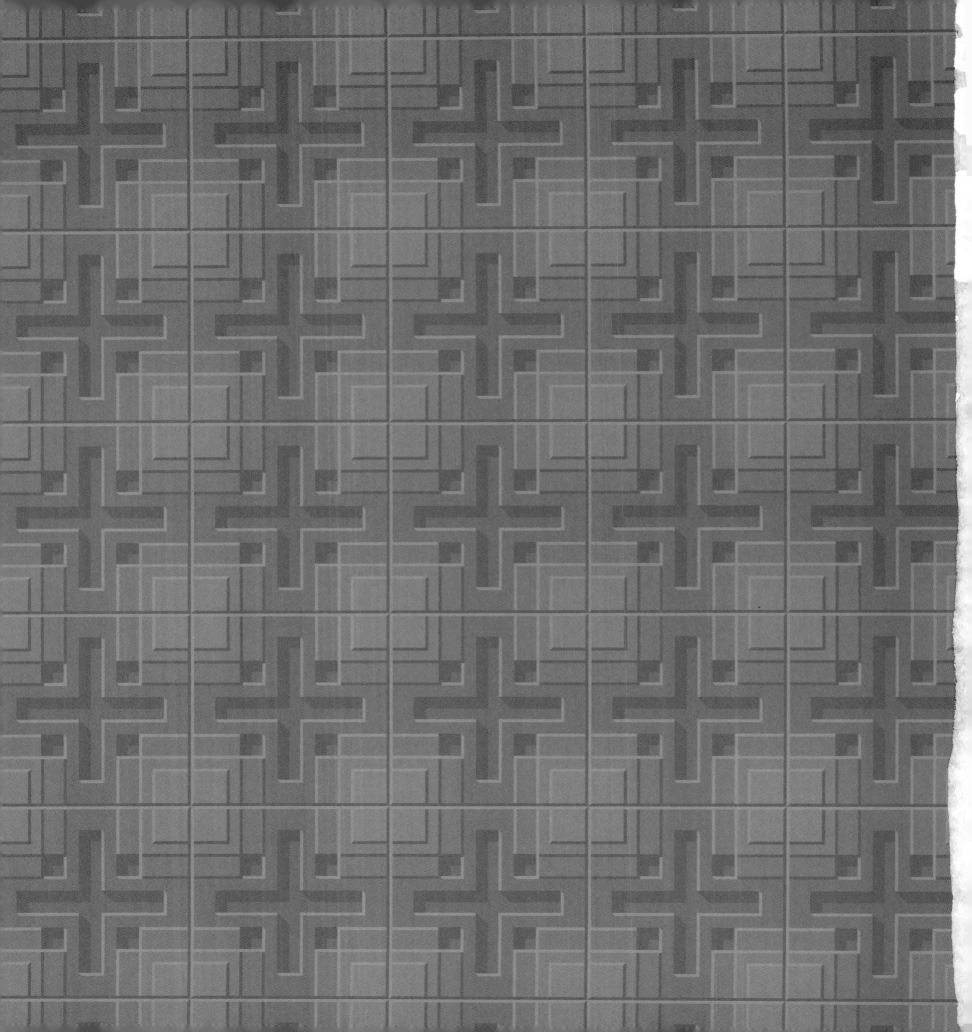

50 FAVOURITE HOUSES BY FRANK LLOYD WRIGHT

DIANE MADDEX

Thames & Hudson

First published in the United Kingdom
in 2000 by Thames & Hudson Ltd,
181A High Holborn, London WC1V 7QX

British Library Cataloguing-in-Publication Data
A catalogue record for this book is available
from the British Library

ISBN 0-500-01992-4

Printed in Singapore

Produced by Archetype Press, Inc.,
Washington, D.C.
Diane Maddex, Project Director
Robert L. Wiser, Designer
Carol Kim, Editorial Assistant

This book was composed in Bernhard Gothic,
designed by Lucian Bernhard, and Wade Sans,
designed by Paul Hickson.

Endpapers and chapter dividers: Adaptation of
a concrete-block pattern used at La Miniatura
(1923) in Pasadena, California, one of four
similar houses designed by Frank Lloyd Wright
in the Los Angeles area in the early 1920s.
Drawing by Robert L. Wiser, Archetype Press.

Page 2: Cedar Rock (1946) in Quasqueton,
Iowa, designed by Frank Lloyd Wright for
Lowell and Agnes Walter.

INTRODUCTION

Frank Lloyd Wright was an architect of houses. In a long lifetime that began just after the Civil War and ended in the space age, he designed an amazing array of buildings—from chicken coops to cathedrals, he liked to boast. But houses became his knottiest challenge and remain his greatest legacy. Wright saw the home as a symbol of American democracy, a monument to individualism more stirring even than a skyscraper. To him it was not merely a place of refuge and family togetherness; one's home was a foundation on which to build a simpler, more honest society. If a nation's architecture—to Wright, the greatest art of any civilization—had integrity, he reasoned, so would its people.

A domestic revolution was afoot when Wright, born June 8, 1867, in Richland Center, Wisconsin, began his career in 1887 as a nineteen-year-old apprentice in Chicago. Before he was thirty, his progressive ideas and his lifelong penchant for expressing them had placed him on the front lines of the campaign to change ingrained habits of living. Distressed with the Victorian era's architectural and cultural excesses, citizens from ministers to married women, politicians to planners, workers to writers all coalesced to remake the home as the first step in revolutionizing society. Out would go dust-catching furnishings that bred germs, labor-intensive work that kept women captive at home, visual disorder that confused children. In would come fewer rooms and simpler materials, compact built-ins, time-saving new technology, more uniformity in house designs to eliminate destructive competition with the neighbors. Wright absorbed these ideas, melded them with a deep love of nature learned as a boy in Wisconsin and a fascination with geometry encouraged by his mother, and emerged with "dress reform" houses as modern as the new woman's clothing. People soon took notice that the stays had been loosened.

After apprenticing briefly in 1887 with Joseph Lyman Silsbee, an architect and family friend in Chicago, the next year Wright began a nearly six-year association with Louis Sullivan, the city's most forward-thinking practitioner. Sullivan did not want to be bothered with houses; his chief draftsman did, even designing a half dozen at home by "moonlight" to make more money as much as to try his hand at this new symbol of American life. The opportunity to specialize came his way quickly when Sullivan, having learned of Wright's verboten work, terminated his employment in 1893. Twenty-six-years old, the young architect launched himself into the world of architecture. From then until his death on April 9, 1959, he invited himself into homes everywhere with principles that have radically reshaped ideas of how people can live.

Wright began to publicly articulate his vision for the modern home the year after he parted from his *"Lieber Meister."* In 1894 he traveled to suburban Evanston, Illinois, to give the University Guild some "golden rules for house building." A house, he admonished, should grow from its site, just as a plant grows from the soil—to produce a truly "organic" architecture. It should be simple and contain as few rooms as possible but never a parlor, that "vaudeville stage" saved for company. Family life should be centered around the living room hearth, and where one sleeps should be equally pleasant. Proportion and harmonious relationships among rooms should be minded, cautioned Wright. Things with no real use or meaning should be avoided. "Go to Nature.... Go to the woods for your color schemes and not the ribbon counter at 'Field's,'" he lectured. Furnishings should be built in, and decoration should be limited to "one really fine thing," perhaps flowers or dried weeds. "Vicious" furniture, bric-a-brac with a notion-store

Wright's home (1889–98) in Oak Park, Illinois, his first house to be built

look, and "unsanitary" draperies all should be avoided. Consistency brings harmony, "good for sore eyes and tired nerves," he added. Do all this, concluded Wright, for the children if for no one else. Because young people breathe in the atmosphere of their home, said this eventual father of seven, where they live should exemplify the same truth, beauty, and consistency their parents teach them verbally. Simplicity and repose were not just ideals to Wright; he saw them as part of homeowners' responsibility to raise the character of their homes.

Wright elaborated on these ideas in another talk in 1896, walking listeners through a more detailed vision of a perfect home from the front steps up to the rooftop and down to the rug on the floor. By then he had already completed about thirty commissions: new houses, remodeled houses, and apartment buildings, including a cottage for himself and his wife, Catherine, in Oak Park, an up-and-coming town outside Chicago that was to serve as a proving ground for his ideas. When he died two months shy of his ninety-second birthday, with yet another house beginning to take shape, Wright had sketched out some four hundred designs for living, three-fourths of which were built (he joked that he just shook them out of his sleeve). During these seven active decades, Wright stated and restated the precepts for a harmonious home that he first propounded in 1894. Those ideals, in fact, reached a much wider audience when they were published in *Architectural Record* in 1908. In other magazine features and in talks, correspondence, and books such as his first and second autobiographies in 1932 and 1943 and *The Natural House*, published in 1954, Wright continued to preach his sermon that the home was the true cathedral of the modern age.

From his first house in 1889 (his own) to his last in 1959, the look of Wright's houses changed—but never the underlying principles. "There should be as many types of homes," he said in 1894, "as there are types of people." Character was to come from the individuality of the occupants—not to mention the artistic genius of their architect. The half dozen "bootleg" houses produced while he was working for Sullivan are a curious mix of forms and historical styles that Wright was simultaneously beginning to sneer at. By way of later explanation, he asserted that he did not try anything radical at the time because it would be too obviously ascribed to him, the surreptitious moonlighter. The years 1893 to 1900 saw more experimentation but also real breakthroughs as Wright redrew walls, windows, and roofs and began to eliminate basements and attics. In 1900 the thirty-three-year-old designer took command of the revolution on the home front with Prairie houses hugging the ground, free-flowing interiors, walls of glass that brought nature indoors, and roofs as sheltering as the trees outside. Wright succeeded in destroying the boxes in which people previously thought they had to live. His love of new technology combined in the 1920s with his search for inexpensive ways to build, and in the 1930s his vision soared over both water and desert to create world-renowned landmarks such as Fallingwater and Taliesin West. In his last two decades Wright struggled to solve the most difficult housing problem of his life: how to build a palace on a schoolteacher's salary. His answer was a house simpler to build and simpler to live in, fit for a reinvigorated country he renamed Usonia.

"I believe a house is more a home by being a work of Art," Wright announced in 1954 in *The Natural House*. To make each one as beautiful as any painting or sculpture was "the modern American opportunity," he had said in 1910, and this belief remained his first principle. Close behind in Wright's conception of organic architecture was the idea that a house must be built with nature, evolving in freedom like a tree. Design should come from within a building, said Wright, rather than being imposed from without by an arbitrary style. A house thus became for him "livable interior space under ample shelter." To be considered a work of art, each house, he added, needed a "grammar of its own," a unified language of architecture. For Wright this came from geometry, which allowed him to weave together buildings as if they were fabric. He preferred nature's colors—especially to recall a forest in the autumn—and natural materials—particularly wood—used naturally. The simplicity of a wildflower or a Japanese woodblock print appealed to him as a model for creating repose at home. Ornament was to be built in, not applied; pattern was to be integral, not merely surface decoration. Furnishings were to be considered part of the whole, as minor elements of the architecture.

Consistency, unity, harmony, integrity—these were Wright's building blocks, and they gave birth to features that changed the idea of home. To him we owe open floor plans with expansive vistas, bands of windows that break down the barrier between inside and out, the dignity of a plain wall, the simplicity of interiors furnished with a single vision, new ways to use (and hide) technology, even the carport to properly house the new modern necessity. The American home, Wright prophesied in 1896, "will be a product of our time, spiritually and physically. It will be a great work of art, respected the world over, because of its integrity, its real worth." In three hundred houses over seventy years, he hurtled many obstacles to make this wish come true.

Wright in the late 1950s at Taliesin West, his desert retreat in Arizona

EARLY

A Shingle-style home for himself, an Italian palazzo in the Windy City, Queen Anne towers, Tudor half-timbering, remodeled Victorians— Wright tried them all in the fifty commissions that came to him during his first dozen years as an architect. Not only was he struggling to find forms to express his ideas, he did not yet carry the authority to insist that

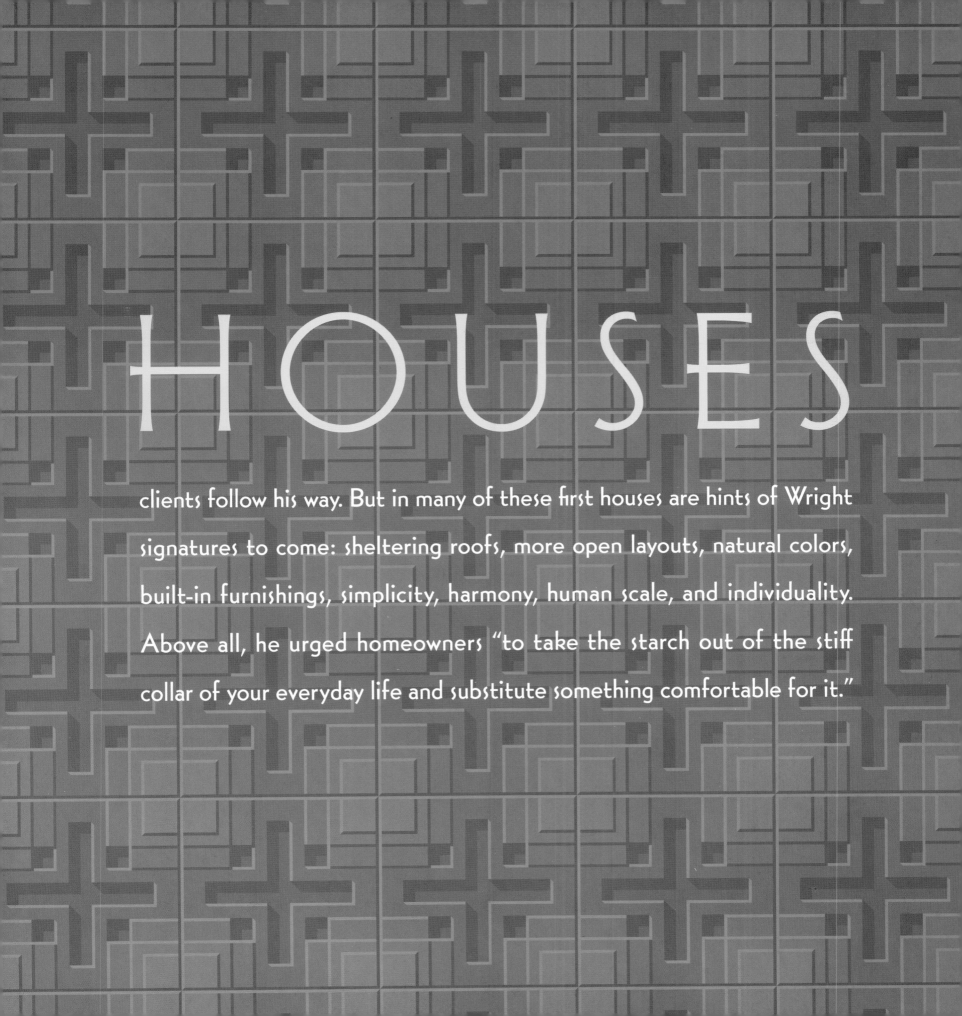

HOUSES

clients follow his way. But in many of these first houses are hints of Wright signatures to come: sheltering roofs, more open layouts, natural colors, built-in furnishings, simplicity, harmony, human scale, and individuality. Above all, he urged homeowners "to take the starch out of the stiff collar of your everyday life and substitute something comfortable for it."

FRANK LLOYD WRIGHT HOME AND STUDIO

For Wright's first house, he had possibly the most demanding client of all: himself. He borrowed money from his employer, Louis Sullivan, to build a shingled cottage in the pleasant Chicago suburb of Oak Park in 1889–90. The young architect complained that the typical house of the day was little more than "a bedeviled box with a fussy lid" punctuated by holes for going in and seeing out. Anything but fussy, the overscaled gable Wright chose was just dramatic enough to set it apart from his late-Victorian neighbors. Yet it was a house that adopted the Queen Anne style's fondness for a potpourri of shapes as well as the Shingle style's rusticity. Wood shingles cover the gable and walls as tightly as skin on bones. Knowing passersby, however, can discern the geometry that was to govern all of Wright's work: triangles, rectangles, circles and semicircles, diamonds in the windows, octagonal bays. The first floor remains mysteriously in the shadows, its entrance door off-center. Wright, who had a small studio behind the second-story windows, enlarged and reshaped his simple home in 1895, changing the kitchen into an autumnal-hued dining room whose projection on the house's right side mirrored his earlier octagonal motif and broke the tyranny of four square walls. Upstairs, Catherine Wright had a sunny day room and their six children were enticed into a barrel-vaulted, lilliputian-scaled playroom lined with art glass. Three years later Wright made another change when he added a complete studio for his growing architectural practice. Visiting the family in February 1897, *House Beautiful* magazine suggested that the architect's house "outside is of no particular character" but admitted that "it has attained a very comfortable and livable appearance." Wright left his home and family in 1909, returning in 1911 only to convert the house into income-earning apartments and to install his wife and children in the studio where he had led an architectural revolution. Today his first home has been restored to its appearance in 1909, when it was Wright's own laboratory.

CHARNLEY HOUSE

Louis Sullivan was fortunate that the chief draftsman
for his firm Adler and Sullivan preferred houses to skyscrapers
(Sullivan's forte). Wright was enlisted in 1891 to design an
urban residence in Chicago for James Charnley. Planning for
the World's Columbian Exposition, to be held in the city in
1893, was under way, and a Renaissance revival was in the air
despite Sullivan's search for a modern architectural language.
Wright gave their lumberman client a brick-and-stone palazzo
hiding eloquent essays in wood inside. Classically inspired—
even mimicking a classical column with its three horizontal
layers of base, center shaft, and capital on top—Charnley's
house was nonetheless exceptionally free of typical Renaissance embellishment. Wright was still tied to the age-old
concept of starting with flat walls, he later explained, but
here he tried to turn a plain facade into its own decoration
through devices such as "a well-placed single opening."
The door, seemingly cut from the stone base, and most of
the windows peer out starkly without decorative surrounds.
A loggia that would be at home in Florence marks the house's
center and adds a welcome void to the solidity of the walls.
The interior layout broke little new ground, although it clearly
grew from the exterior's three vertical divisions. The Victorian
era's love of ornate wood trim lingers inside. Wright would
soon eliminate trim from his design vocabulary but not before
producing a lacy spindled screen that rises high to add fluctua-
ting light to the stairwell. In his hands wood became "plastic . . .
light and continuously flowing instead of the prevailing heavy
'cut and butt' carpenter work," he recollected in 1954. Sullivanesque ornament outside and in mixes with the evolving
rectilinear forms that would become Wright's hallmark.
The Society of Architectural Historians, appropriately, now
maintains its headquarters in this sculptural block of a house.

WINSLOW HOUSE

By 1893 Wright had made the break from working for others to working toward his ideal of the American home. William H. Winslow of the neighboring suburb of River Forest, Illinois, stepped forward as Wright's first client after his departure from Adler and Sullivan. Dressed in the golden hues of a prairie autumn, the Winslow House shows the same classical lineage as James Charnley's house—but with a difference pointing the way to Wright's future. Here the architect took as his metaphor not a classical column but a tree rooted in nature. Rising from a low water table tying it to the ground, the Roman-brick villa is ringed by a leafy terra-cotta frieze and sheltered by a broad roof as protective as overhanging branches. It burst on the scene, he said in his 1932 *Auto-biography*, "like a Prima Vera in full bloom." Wright regarded this house as the beginning of his Prairie period. The layered facade was still symmetrical, and the windows were still scattered across it, but the twenty-six-year-old architect was beginning to express the sweep of the prairie and the sense of shelter encompassed in the idea of home. With its swirling Sullivanesque ornament, the dark second-story band was a backward nod to his mentor, but it allowed Wright to make this part of the wall almost disappear. The hipped roof, a symbol of freedom, hovers magically above the house's clearly articulated face. More floral ornament, reminiscent of an 1892 Sullivan-designed tomb, rings the front door and its flanking windows like eyeglass frames and spills over onto the door itself, a pert mouth calling visitors to enter. The restrained front gives way in the rear to a cacophony of projected spaces, as if Wright were punching his way out of flat walls. A walled stable-garage, in which the owner and the architect handprinted their book *The House Beautiful* beginning in 1896, telegraphs the fluid Prairie plans and shapes that were soon to emerge from Wright's drafting board. Neoclassical arches in the porte cochere and stable tower and, inside, in the entry-hall inglenook and passageways, however, testify to Wright's reluctance to jettison all historic architectural motifs—yet.

MOORE HOUSE

Not all of Wright's early clients shared his evolving vision of
what modern architecture should be. A number of the houses
designed during his first decade as an architect, in fact, seem
to owe more to the "frozen" styles of the past than to any new
way of building. In the half dozen "bootleg" houses created
after hours while he was working for Louis Sullivan and in
some of the independent commissions that followed, Wright
moved from variants of Dutch and English colonial to Queen
Anne and Tudor. He rationalized this riot of styles by asserting
in 1894 that Americans' individuality demanded different
types of homes for different types of people. For their corner
lot in Oak Park on the same street as Wright's own home,
Nathan and Anna Moore pictured an English Tudor complete
with half-timbering in the gables. Wright's 1895 design using
narrow Roman brick gave them what they wanted, with an
open porch and a few other Wrightian embellishments. But
after a fire at Christmas in 1922 burned the top of the house,
Wright returned and remade the Moores' home more to his
own liking. Where half-timbering had etched a traditional
medieval pattern on the original gables, the emboldened
architect inserted his own abstracted motifs. Windows were
extended high into the gables, a vertical lift accentuated by
tall chimneys that sliced through the roofs. New decorative
features showed Wright's fascination at the time with Meso-
american, Japanese, and other exotic art forms. Although the
Moore House remains a perplexing hybrid, Wright was soon to
change both his focus and the balance of power between client
and architect. There were to be no more Tudors or Colonial
Revivals or any other "tombs of a life that has been lived," only
what Wright thought best for the new American lifestyle.

HELLER HOUSE

With the Heller House of 1896 Wright's idea of what a home
should be finally took shape in brick and mortar. Gone was
the house of old that would "rear on its hind legs and paw
the air in order that you may seem more important than your
neighbor," as he said disdainfully in 1894. In its place was
"simplicity and repose," molded into rectilinear lines that echo
Isidore Heller's narrow urban property in Chicago. From its
layers of overhanging roofs and bold exterior mien to its open
living areas inside, this house announces the Prairie houses to
come in just a few years. The entrance, set apart with Sullivanesque stonework, is somewhat hidden on the side, about a
third of the way down the long lot. Walking up short flights of
steps and along the path, visitors have time to contemplate
what awaits them. In the hall green and bronze walls framed in
wood create the aura of a wooded glen and lead on the right
to the living room and on the left to the dining room, both
warmed by fireplaces. These two rooms are cruciform, or cross-
shaped, a plan type that later became the basis for many of
Wright's Prairie houses. The Heller House rises to three stories,
its height mitigated with a hipped roof over the second floor
that serves as a base for a colonnaded third story housing a
playroom. Ringing this level is a terra-cotta frieze of dancing
beauties created for Wright by the sculptor Richard Bock.
With solid walls replaced by artful voids, the top roof thus
appears to float above, much like at the Winslow House.
Windows are grouped in threes, fours, and fives rather than
randomly cut out of the walls. With this dramatic change,
Wright noted in 1954, "I was working away at the wall as
a wall and bringing it towards the function of a screen...."

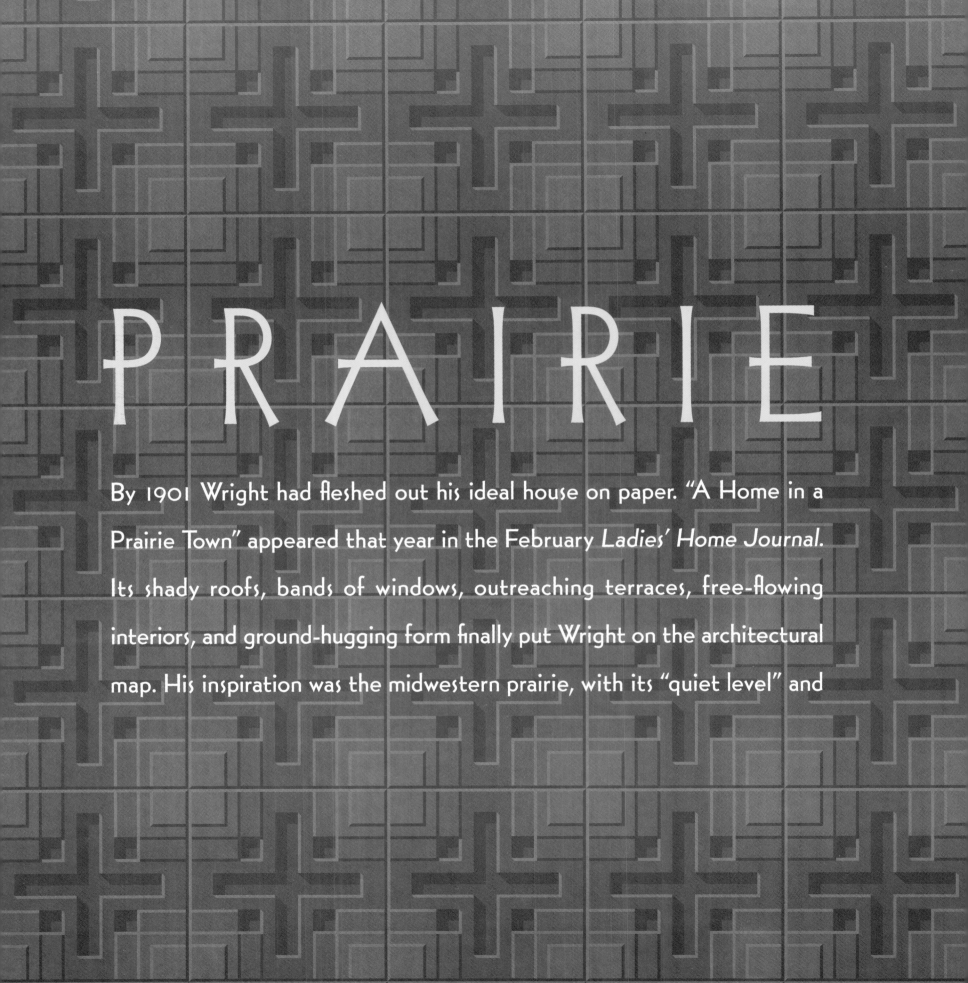

PRAIRIE

By 1901 Wright had fleshed out his ideal house on paper. "A Home in a Prairie Town" appeared that year in the February *Ladies' Home Journal.* Its shady roofs, bands of windows, outreaching terraces, free-flowing interiors, and ground-hugging form finally put Wright on the architectural map. His inspiration was the midwestern prairie, with its "quiet level" and

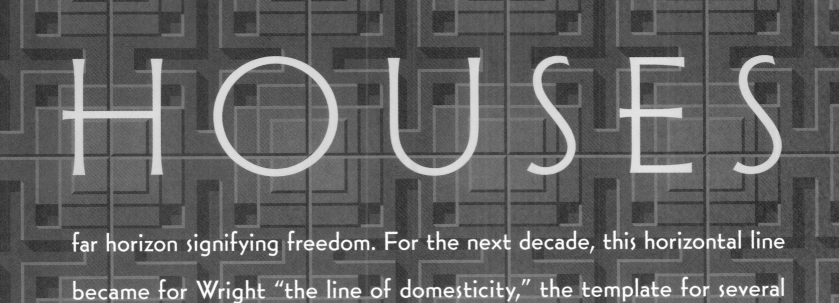

HOUSES

far horizon signifying freedom. For the next decade, this horizontal line became for Wright "the line of domesticity," the template for several hundred designs (about 120 of which were built). He furnished his Prairie houses with shimmering art glass, prominent hearths, and custom furniture in the colors of nature, making each home a harmonious work of art.

THOMAS HOUSE

Not the first of Wright's Prairie houses, this was the first to go
up in his hometown of Oak Park. In two designs the previous
year—the Bradley and Hickox Houses of 1900 in Kankakee,
Illinois—the thirty-three-year-old architect had finally devised
a house type he thought was right for modern American
living. When James Rogers asked Wright to create a home
in Oak Park for his daughter and son-in-law, Frank Thomas,
the new local celebrity responded in 1901 with a brilliant
jewel that set the look for the emerging Prairie style. Wright
dissolved solid walls by combining windows filled with art
glass into broad screens of light. He raised the main living area
of the three-story residence to the second floor, eliminating
the need for a damp basement. Stucco walls, which hid
the servants' quarters, enclose a terrace and are married
to the ground with only a low water table. A cavelike arched
gateway changes the geometric theme while it outlines
a convoluted route to the main entrance, a bower of
luminescent green-and-white glass, on the second level.
Overhead, gently hipped roofs intersect in a protective
embrace. Even more important was the revolution inside.
Wright's Prairie houses abandoned the old, confining foursquare and center-hall plans; in their place came more open
cruciform and pinwheel arrangements that helped bring down
the walls inside just as they were falling away outside. Here
Wright used basically an L shape, the living room along the
facade divided from the projecting dining room and breakfast
nook by the hall and kitchen. But once the roofs and long
entryway are considered, the design begins to look more like
a pinwheel that spins around the hearth buried deep in the
living room. Four bedrooms are lined up on the uppermost
level, sheltered by the eaves and secluded from the street,
private yet open with generous windows. Barely two blocks
down the street from his own 1889 home, the Thomas House
was light years away in expressing the unfolding space within—by then Wright's most challenging architectural concern.

FRICKE HOUSE

If the horizontal was Wright's new line of domesticity, the Fricke House of 1901 in Oak Park seems to be a detour in his quest for the prairie. Wings stretch out to touch nature but then rise up in the center to a three-story section that towers over the outreaching sides. This vertical-on-horizontal tension recalls Wright's elaborate Husser House of 1899 (demolished in 1926) and the tall-yet-broad Heller House from 1896, both nearby in Chicago, as well as the eclectic Rollin Furbeck House of 1897 also in Oak Park. Encircling wood bands on the stucco walls, soon to become a Prairie-style hallmark, underscore both dimensions of the house. Perhaps Wright sought to give the Frickes a belvedere from which to survey the still-rustic charms of Oak Park as well as their own patch of paradise at the back of their lot. There, on the house's private side, he erected a roofed garden pavilion that could be viewed from the dining and living areas and was reached by a covered walkway. Although this distinctive structure was razed in 1928 to make way for a neighboring house, Wright clearly intended to bring together nature and architecture and to entice the residents out of their home. A built-in porch opens off the kitchen on the house's left side, while balconies and a terrace bring light and air to the second-story bedrooms. From the triangular reception room at ground level up to the billiard room in the tower, geometrically patterned art glass etches the windows with delicate tracery. The second owner, Emma Martin, called Wright back to add a matching two-story garage to the property in 1907 (he had designed the house originally with his brief and only partner, Webster Tomlinson). House, pavilion, and garage all made for a cohesive if transitional statement in Wright's new architectural language.

WILLITS HOUSE

Few people would disagree with Wright that this was his first great Prairie house. The profile in league with the ground, the intersecting hipped roofs, the bands of art glass windows, the walled terrace—it all came together perfectly here in 1902 on Sheridan Road in the far Chicago suburb of Highland Park. Ward and Cecilia Willits, who became friends of the architect and his wife, received a plan developed from the second of two model houses by Wright published in the *Ladies' Home Journal* in 1901. Although this one was entitled "A Small House with 'Lots of Room in It,'" the Willits version exudes a feeling of roominess enhanced by the open spaces inside. Wood screens take over from solid walls to subtly divide the major living areas, inviting tantalizing glimpses of rooms beyond. The extended arms of the cruciform plan enabled Wright to clothe two or three sides of a room with light; the old sense of being in a box evaporated in full sunlight. At the second story, windows hug the overhanging eaves and make the wall disappear more successfully than did the frieze on the Winslow House. Wright has moved the door, however, from center front to a secluded spot on the right side, near the cantilevered porte cochere. To the left of the living room, projected toward the street in a neighborly gesture, an extended veranda and covered porch off the dining room complete the cross. Triangular bays on the front and end help the dining room reach further out to nature. Layers of roofs glide over the stucco walls like birds on the prairie; corners on the second floor have flown away. Low walls provide privacy while they link the whole composition. As satisfying a piece of architecture as this was, it was not enough to preserve Wright's friendship with the Willitses. They fell out after the couple joined the Wrights on their first trip to Japan in 1905.

HEURTLEY HOUSE

Wright found the raised house plan "especially suited to the prairie" and used it again in 1902 just up Forest Avenue from the Thomas House in Oak Park. Living room, dining room, kitchen, pantry, and three bedrooms moved upstairs for the best views. To the right a covered loggia opening off the living room and master bedroom heightens the sense of residing in the treetops. The ground floor originally housed a large playroom, guest rooms, servants' quarters, storage, and its own loggia and terrace to bring the out-of-doors inside. As with the Thomas House, an arch directs the way inside via a cavelike entrance; here it hides behind a low wall whose triangular point contrasts playfully with a rotund urn and the circular and rectilinear lines of the house itself. Most striking of all are the walls. Alternately receding and projecting, courses of warm red and lighter brick rise to turn the surface into its own ornament. Wright let the masonry be what it wanted to be. Two piers stop well short of the roof, demonstrating that it can float freely without visible means of support. Because Wright eliminated the attic, his roofs did not need to threaten the sky with high peaks; lower and covering all, they became a more potent symbol of shelter. Light in color, the roof's undersides reflect light back inside, where Wright used "ribbons" of wood bands like plastic to mark the rise of the tented ceiling. Announcing the hearth at the house's center, a single broad chimney anchors this "quiet skyline" directly to the earth.

33

DANA-THOMAS HOUSE

In Susan Lawrence Dana of Springfield, Illinois, Wright finally found a client to feed his dreams. Beginning in 1902 he designed this wealthy widow a prairie palace suitable for entertaining the local royalty. He was called in to enlarge Dana's Italianate family home, but by the time he finished little more than one identifiable room remained. No one missed the old place, because Wright produced a romantic essay in vaulted spaces, glistening glass, custom furnishings, and sheer bravado never equalled in his residential repertoire. A seemingly upward lilt to the copper-edged roofs shows his continuing fascination with Japan, while beneath it a copper-like plaster frieze tinted verdigris green seems to be another holdover from his days with Louis Sullivan; its stylized pattern of leaves, squares, and lightning streaks echoes the roof shape and other elements of the house itself. The nearly block-long villa of creamy Roman brick rises two stories over a basement and stretches along a glassed-in conservatory from the living areas to a monumental studio designed for "the artistic activities of the community"; a library descends below ground. Space unfolds in the soaring entry hall to invite visitors up to the major public rooms, giving them "a thrill of welcome" as Wright liked. The two-story dining room, crowned with an oak-ribbed barrel vault, enveloped diners in the hues of autumn leaves and a prairie-flower mural by George Mann Niedecken to match. Taking his cue from prairie sumac, Wright wove geometric abstractions throughout the house in hundreds of windows and doors, sconces and table lamps. Butterflies flutter near the entrance in circular transoms of art glass and dangle from the ceiling in hanging lamps. Sculpture, both classical and new, underscores the three-dimensionality of the grand house, now a museum owned by the State of Illinois. It is a prairie feast that looks inward, rather than out to its city neighborhood, to find nature in Wright's own imagination. Dana's house was a showcase for the architect's percolating ideas, but its opulent scale makes it a one-of-a-kind example. For a man whose fame was to come from trying to house the average American family, it was a rare indulgence.

DARWIN MARTIN HOUSE

Most of Wright's clients during his Prairie years were business people who seemed as willing to take chances with their architecture as with their professional affairs. Darwin Martin of Buffalo, New York, encountered Wright through his brother William Martin, whose Oak Park home was designed by the architect in 1902. Darwin Martin signed on with Wright not only for an extraordinary new company headquarters— the Larkin Administration Building of 1903, now demolished— but also for his own home, a summer retreat, and a Chicago factory; his sister built a Wright home adjacent to her brother's lot. It was a family of patrons for a man who always needed them. Wright returned the favor in 1904 with one of his most assured Prairie houses. Darwin and Isabel Martin were as fond of nature as Wright, so he set their red brick house into a paradise of his own making, an antidote to Buffalo's long winters. From the entry, hothouse splendors beckoned just past the dining room, down a long brick-and-glass pergola that provided safe passage to a conservatory filled with greenery. Gardens on either side brought the outdoors in. Within and without, Wright had achieved a synthesis of architecture and nature—so that, as he said in 1896, "you scarcely know where ground leaves off and building begins." The Martins' garden structures are gone now, torn down in 1959 along with their garage. Also lost over time was a wisteria-mosaic fireplace, but nature still makes itself known throughout the house, most famously in its Tree of Life windows. These art glass patterns, stylized stand-ins for the real thing, energize the casement windows that ring the walls. Swinging outward to embrace the outdoors, their clear panes allowed Wright to work his wizardry uninterrupted by mullions and muntins. The upper walls vanish under the eaves in a leaf-filled screen of light. Although tall, the house's center section eases into horizontality by stepping down toward the ground with overlapping hipped roofs. A concrete pagoda of a birdhouse and Wright's signature circle-in-square concrete planters keep nature close to this home far away from the prairie where it all began.

COONLEY HOUSE

Avery and Queene Coonley of Riverside, Illinois, were
two other devoted Wright clients who came back for more.
Queene Coonley, in fact, told Wright that they saw in his
work "the countenances of principle." For the stuccoed
suburban villa he designed for them in 1906, he returned to
one of his key principles—nature—and produced a roughly
U-shaped courtyard structure that wrapped its arms around
the landscape. As in some of his previous Prairie houses, life
in the Coonleys' home took place mainly on the second story.
The living, dining, and kitchen areas were separated by a
study from the private zone holding three bedrooms. Guest
rooms formed an arm on one side, servants' rooms on the other.
From the elevated living room, its tented ceiling a canopy
of wooden beams, the family could look out through art glass
windows onto a large pool that reflected the house's image
back to them. Perforated-wood panels, murals, skylights, built-
in and freestanding furniture, and custom textiles all made it
seem a Wrightian wonderland. His continuing fascination with
integral ornament—"wrought in the warp and woof of the
structure"—took form here in a colorful exterior wall frieze.
Its square pattern punctuated by orange, gold, white, and blue
tile found counterparts in the Coonley windows and gave a
taste of exotic motifs to come at Midway Gardens (1913) in
Chicago, the Imperial Hotel (1916–22) in Tokyo, and Wright's
concrete-block houses in California (1923). Sunken gardens,
a gardener's cottage, and a coach house filled out the rest of
the wooded estate, one that tripped on its grand scale after
the Coonleys moved east. In the 1950s the property was split
to accommodate five families where one had lived originally.
As part of their legacy as Wright clients, the Coonleys left
another building: their famous 1912 playhouse (a progressive
kindergarten) in Riverside, which has since been adapted
as a residence, opening its doors for new Wright homeowners.

38

ROBIE HOUSE

A great ship of brick slicing through the landscape, the Robie House has come to symbolize Wright's Prairie houses: the essence of shelter, its intersecting planes frozen like music. It was his first *Dampfer* house, he said—a steamship, as his German admirers called it. Behind the sweeping red decks lived not sailors but the family of a bicycle manufacturer who loved inventiveness as much as Wright. Frederick Robie knew what he wanted in a house even before he found the perfect architect. It was "one of those Wright houses," everyone told him. For Robie's wide but shallow corner lot near the University of Chicago, Wright in 1908 gave him what both wanted. Although three stories high, the house's low profile remains an ode to the flat land. A daringly cantilevered roof reaches out at each end far beyond any obvious means of support, which comes from steel buried inside rather than from the low brick piers and walls that only pretend to hold it up. Raised to the middle level to capture a view over the old Midway, the living area is essentially one long room; only a two-sided brick hearth announces where the living room ends and the dining room begins. Triangular "prows" are the lookouts. The front rectangle holding the main rooms passes another shiplike rectangle that sequesters the kitchen and service areas. Overhead, edged by a broad chimney, a compact belvedere provided sleeping quarters for the captain and crew. Between the entry court and garage at ground level stood a playroom for the two children. Walls extending to the property line provided privacy plus security while they energized the entire composition where verticals met horizontals. Tucked under the shady overhangs, bands of art glass windows invited views out but kept others from looking in. Before this *magnum opus* was finished, Wright departed Oak Park for a yearlong sojourn in Europe. George Niedecken, an "interior architect" from Milwaukee who furnished a handful of Wright's Prairie houses, took over inside. But a little more than a year after all was ready for the Robie family in 1910, Lora Robie left her new house with her children, and by the end of 1911 Frederick Robie's grand invention had been sold.

MAY HOUSE

Wright was beginning to feel "weary," burdened by every-
thing, most of all "domesticity"—an ironic state of affairs for
an architect who celebrated the cult of family life. Yet in
1908, his last full year of work in the Oak Park studio, he
turned out a handful of mature houses that summed up the
Prairie style. One of the most well known of these, because
of its recent meticulous restoration, is the Grand Rapids,
Michigan, home of Meyer and Sophie May. The house
commands its lot in a tight T shape, calling attention to its
front terrace. Piers of tan brick filled with dazzling art glass
frame the living room to the left; copper work weaves them
together and proclaims the square as the house's geometric
motif. On the bedroom level above, more patterned windows
make the walls disappear; Wright has even turned the corners,
freed from having to lift the roof, into glass boxes. Inside,
space flows effortlessly with the help of open wood screens
in lieu of solid dividers. An assertive brick fireplace pointed
with golden glass commands the far side of the living
room, a rare instance in which Wright placed the hearth
on an outside wall rather than at the center of the house.
Occupying that space in the May House is a broad pier
encircled in hollyhocks: a silvery mural created by George
Niedecken. It suffuses the modest home with light rather
than heat and allowed the family to dine surrounded by
nature, real and man-made. Niedecken completed the fully
coordinated furnishings during Wright's absence and returned,
as the family grew to include two children, to add others.
Sophie May died prematurely in 1917, but her husband lived
on in their perfect Prairie house until his death in 1936.

ISABEL ROBERTS HOUSE

Showing his perpetual inventiveness, even when worked
out, Wright in 1908 completed a very different house for his
bookkeeper, Isabel Roberts. Located in the suburb of River
Forest adjacent to Oak Park, the small house forecasts designs
to come from Wright's hand three decades later. Low, sweeping roofs that characterized his Usonian houses of the 1930s
and beyond settle gently here on a typical Prairie cruciform
plan. To the left, alongside the entrance, diamond-paned
windows turn the dining room into an enchanting bower.
A perforated-wood screen showers more light down onto the
dining table. The living room takes its place in the front arm
of the cross plan. Across the room from a cavelike hearth, glass
rises the full two stories to demolish all sense of confining walls.
It is the kind of contrast—light and dark, open and closed—
that drove Wright's best work. Eliminating the ceiling as well
as the walls, he ringed the living room with a balcony so that
upstairs and downstairs also merged as one. To the right a
projecting porch made room in its hipped roof for an old elm
tree that has been appropriately pampered over the years.
Originally finished in stucco, the house was bricked over in
the 1920s and then upgraded inside by Wright himself in 1955,
four years before his death. He replaced less expensive pine
paneling with more modern blonde mahogany, added copper
to the roofs, and reconfigured some of the rooms. That it was
able to accommodate the changes—like the roof its living
tree—is further proof that Wright built his buildings on
enduring principles rather than on styles of the moment.

44

LAURA GALE HOUSE

Premonitions of things to come can be felt in another house for another single-woman client. Laura Gale was actually the widow of Thomas Gale when her new Oak Park house was built in 1909. The Gales were among Wright's select group of repeat clients: he designed a "bootleg" house for them in 1892 not far from his own home, then a summer cottage in 1897 in Whitehall, Michigan, followed by three rental cottages a decade later in the same resort. Laura Gale's new home for herself and her two children nearly shocked the neighbors, who should no longer have been surprised by what Wright built in their town. Arrayed under a flat roof, the second-floor front balcony and ground-level terrace hover like open bureau drawers, injecting themselves into the landscape. For Wright the cantilever was the the most romantic construction tool available to him, one whose steel underpinnings "afforded boundless new expressions … as free … as a winged bird." With his world-famous Fallingwater in 1935, he perfected his ability to soar over mere earth and water. Wright may have planned to build the new Gale House of concrete, but the wood trim he used rhythmically outlines the stucco walls to further mark their outward thrust. The house unfolds to the side in intersecting planes and dynamic horizontals and verticals. The simple interior plan separates the dining room at the back of the house from the living room by two steps and built-in cabinets that frame the entrance. Doors leading from the terrace invite light into the living areas. Four bedrooms, a bath, and a maid's room fill the upstairs. "Here is the progenitor of Fallingwater," Wright declared in 1951. All that was missing were some boulders, dense woods, and a gentle waterfall.

TALIESIN

By the time Wright returned in late 1910 from his year abroad, his Prairie period was essentially over. He had altered his life in many ways, exchanging his wife and six children for a mistress, Mamah Borthwick Cheney, and garnering accolades for his work in Europe with a German publication featuring his recent buildings. Wright was ready to move on architecturally; with a few exceptions, the Prairie style faded from his design vocabulary. Exotic forms and motifs began to call to him as he started to build a new home and a new life on family land in Spring Green, Wisconsin. Taliesin, begun in 1911, was his "shining brow" (its Welsh translation), built "of the hill," not *on* it. Both the abstract form and the materials of Wright's first "natural house" took their cues from the beloved landscape of his youth. Rustic limestone walls, laid as if still in the quarry, begin in the garden court, clad the open pavilions, and then come indoors to weave inside with outside. Sandy-colored walls recall the valley's riverbanks below, while tented roofs and ceilings mimic the surrounding hills. The "earth-line" governed Wright's architectural horizon as it had in the past decade, but designing his own house—a refuge conceived in romance—allowed him unprecedented freedom to build "broad shelter seeking fellowship with its surroundings." Taliesin eventually grew to be a six-hundred-acre gentleman's estate encompassing farm buildings, a dam and power house, an 1896 windmill (named Romeo and Juliet), family houses, and his architectural school and drafting room located in a 1902 school building designed for his aunts. But in 1914 the first of three fires at Taliesin brought tragedy to Wright's new life. A rampaging servant killed seven persons inside the house and set it ablaze. Mamah Cheney and her two children were among those lost. Showing the fortitude that lasted into his ninety-second year, Wright reinvented himself, rebuilt his "shining brow"—as he had to do again in 1925 and 1952—and went on to show the world how to forge architecture in the flames. "Taliesin!" he wrote in his 1932 *Autobiography*. "When I am away from it, like some rubber band, stretched out but ready to snap back immediately the pull is relaxed or released, I get back to it, happy to be home again."

BOOTH HOUSE

As important as it was to Wright to design a perfect house, he was equally challenged by the need to build enlightened communities. His prototype for "A Home in a Prairie Town" in the February 1901 *Ladies' Home Journal* featured a quadruple block plan for an entire Prairie-style enclave. His ideal home of 1901 was meant not to stand alone but to be one-quarter of a four-part housing grid allowing "breadth and prospect" in the public sphere and privacy for each individual homeowner. This was only one of Wright's early experimental ideas for housing the new America in apartment buildings, workers' dwellings, urban row houses, and suburban villas—most of them never built if not just ignored. When Wright's attorney Sherman Booth asked him in 1911 to develop plans for a community called Ravine Bluffs in the northern Chicago suburb of Glencoe, Wright finally had a real project to address. A bridge over the ravine announces Wright's presence with a tall concrete pylon; sculptures and planters mark boundaries with a mix of circular and rectilinear shapes. At only six houses, rather than two dozen, Ravine Bluffs was never fully realized. Wright designed Booth a stable and garage in 1912, but his client rejected the proposed house, a cousin in plan to Taliesin. Instead, Booth called him back three years later to make the outbuildings into his home. Choosing a form as sculptural as his entrance signs, Wright placed a four-story stucco structure at the juncture of the existing buildings. Now arms spin outward one way for bedrooms, another for the dining room and kitchen, and a third for the living room and its extended "living porch," which bathes the center of the house in light. Wright economized on Booth's rental houses by using one basic square floor plan for four of the five, although he varied their orientation as he had homes in his previous community plans. Different roof shapes, from flat to gabled to hipped, set them apart. A small but early planned community, Ravine Bluffs shows Wright's deep interest in housing people economically but stylishly. Until the end of his career he was to shake even more of these innovations out of his sleeve: prefabricated homes, "automatic" houses, and a whole city of the future.

ALLEN HOUSE

An interior garden or a courtyard allowed Wright to direct a
family's attention inward, toward nature of his own creation.
Lessons he learned at Taliesin, and earlier at the Martin and
Coonley Houses, translated well to the plains of Wichita,
Kansas. There, in 1916, for "as colorful a client as all outdoors,"
Wright brought the outside perpetually inside with a lush
courtyard enclosing a pool. Henry J. Allen was editor of the
Wichita *Beacon*, later the state's governor and U.S. senator,
and then a presidential hopeful. His house bears formal
signatures of the Prairie style, especially in its low, sheltering
roofs, but it benefited from Wright's experimentation at
Taliesin with more natural ways of building. The courtyard
fits neatly into the house's L shape, whose two arms hold the
living and dining rooms between a large terrace. Bedrooms,
a sleeping porch, and Allen's study occupy the long side's
second floor. Greenery from the urban paradise below fills
the windows of the upstairs corridor. In the courtyard, which
terminates in a garden house, the street facade's brick finish
gives way to stucco panels above and brick underneath,
with wood bands added to further delineate the two levels.
As at Taliesin, the basic plan here—a garden or private side
tucked into an ell opposite a public side facing the street—
became the basis for the more modest Usonian houses Wright
launched two decades later. For Wright, Allen was more than
just a client; like Darwin Martin and others, he helped bail the
architect out of trouble. In 1927 Senator Allen interceded to
keep Olgivanna Hinzenberg, Wright's third-wife-to-be and
mother of their child, Iovanna, from being deported. To be a
Wright client was often to sign up for more than just a building.

BOGK HOUSE

When Wright came to design a town house on a narrow lot in Milwaukee in 1916, he turned his gaze from the prairie to Central America and Japan. There were no sweeping vistas as at Taliesin and no room to build around a courtyard. Frederick Bogk's house would have to be its own mountain, make its own ornament. Beginning with the Midway Gardens entertainment complex of 1913 for Chicago, Wright had entered a new, more ornamental phase of his career. A visit to the Panama-California Exposition in California in 1915 and then the commission in 1916 to design the Imperial Hotel for Tokyo heightened his interest in forms more exotic than the prairie had to offer. In 1916 he crowned a sober brick warehouse in Richland Center, Wisconsin, with an immense cornice richly woven of geometric motifs. At the Bogk House Wright transformed this idea into a cast-concrete lintel topping the facade's second-story windows, a device reminiscent of the roofline friezes of his early houses. Here Amerindian chieftains stand guard over the brick cube of a house and frame the central screen of windows, which are enlivened with narrow battlement-like slits of art glass. A widely overhanging hipped roof provides solid cover. Like the Mayans' "earth-architecture: gigantic masses of masonry . . . all planned as one mountain," the design embodied what Wright saw as a primitive and thus natural way of building. In Tokyo, similarly sculptural portions of the Imperial Hotel could have been brothers to the Bogk facade. To preserve the streetside symmetry, the entrance to the foursquare house is to the left. The window-lined dining room at the back, raised three steps above the living room, is a focal point of the first floor. To its side is a glassed-in garden alcove and nearby a goldfish pond. Wright was traveling back and forth between Japan and the United States and had to call once more on George Niedecken to finish the Bogk furnishings. Working together, they added Japanese features: *tokonomas* (built-in alcoves for artwork), caning on the dining room furniture similar to the Imperial Hotel chairs, gilt walls, and small-patterned rug motifs. Infused with the Japanese spirit, the house became Wright's *sayonara* to the prairie.

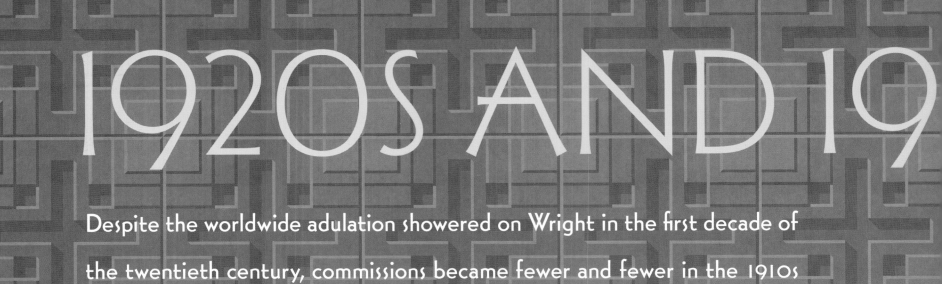

1920S AND 19

Despite the worldwide adulation showered on Wright in the first decade of the twentieth century, commissions became fewer and fewer in the 1910s and 1920s and then worsened as the Great Depression took hold in the 1930s. But, rising like a phoenix from the devastating fire at Taliesin in 1914, the architect reinvented himself with a new sense of freedom.

30S HOUSES

He went on a "California Romanza" in the early 1920s, devising new ways of building with old materials. And in the 1930s, while many inventive projects never moved off his drafting board—"children of imagination," he called them—he created two of the century's most famous houses: one over a waterfall and another a home for himself in the Arizona desert.

HOLLYHOCK HOUSE

If ever there was a place for the courtyard house type that Wright had recently explored, California was it. Where year-round access was limited in Illinois and Wisconsin and Kansas, the Golden State's climate permitted a daily weaving of domestic life with nature. Wright chose this form for the Hollywood house he began designing for Aline Barnsdall in 1917, a project that was not completed until 1921. The oil heiress called it Hollyhock House, after her favorite flower, but its essence is less floral than exotic and primitive. It rises atop Olive Hill as if it were a long-lost relative of the Toltec, Aztec, Mayan, and Inca structures that, recalled Wright in 1957, "stirred my wonder, excited my wishful admiration." Art stone hollyhock effigies dance in a frieze around the roof and reappear on courtyard posts and urns and inside on walls and furniture. The U-shaped stucco house, originally meant to be entirely reinforced concrete, stretches around a garden court lined with a colonnade and pergola. Rooms open onto this shady refuge more than to the sunnier outer side. Water intensifies the sense of coolness, from a square pool off the living room to a circular counterpart at the opposite end of this sprawling, earth-bound structure; a rivulet even flows inside to carve a moat around the fireplace. A theatrical client in every sense, Barnsdall had asked Wright to build not just this house but a complex including theaters, artists' studios, and several residences. Only two other houses were completed, one of which has been demolished. The project was among Wright's most difficult: a client as demanding as he, prolonged absences by both. But he let this new ground speak to him, and he answered with a new architectural language not beholden to Old World concepts of style. Mayan temple or Indian pueblo, it builds on a number of indigenous American forms, abstracting them from native soil to create organic architecture. Wright called it his "Romanza"—freedom to make his own music—a holiday that "traveled the upward road of poetic form." Embellishing the straight line and the flat plane with rhythmic integral ornament, he composed a symphony.

60
:
:
:
:
:
:

LA MINIATURA

Los Angeles continued to work its magic on Wright during the 1920s. In four houses designed in 1923, he found a way to integrate patterns into his buildings as if he were weaving oriental rugs. Wright, in fact, often called himself a weaver. His fabric was concrete, a favorite material of his but one he said in 1928 "has neither song nor story." It was architecture's "gutter rat," but Wright transformed it into uniform blocks that were cast with distinctive patterns and stacked to make walls inside and out. The weaver called them textile blocks. At about sixteen inches square, the blocks provided both the texture and the unit system governing the plan of each house. Form and space were thus united in "an ordered fabric." The first of the quartet to be finished was La Miniatura in Pasadena, commissioned by Alice Millard, a former client who had moved west from Highland Park, Illinois. Wright sited her house too boldly in a ravine subject to flooding. It rises there next to a eucalyptus tree, he said, like a desert cactus— a perfect example of reinforced construction. Unfortunately, Wright's own new building system was not yet perfected, and the textile blocks were laid without steel reinforcements, with only air between interior and exterior walls. Yet the house exerts the mysterious pull of pre-Columbian sculpture, its cross-patterned blocks a clue to its own shape. The dining room and kitchen occupy the ground floor, off a terrace. Above, freed from the horizontal line of the prairie, lies a two-story living room reaching for the stars. A balconied bedroom caps the house. Perforated blocks inviting light inside mix with solid blocks to vary the rhythm of the concrete walls. Wright found the "hitherto unsuspected soul" in this building material by texturing it like the trees he found in California.

63

STORER HOUSE

Wright's second textile-block house, for Dr. John Storer, had
to nestle into the Hollywood hills—a far different challenge
from the flat midwestern prairie. Terraces meld house and
landscape, snaking around the property to open living spaces
to the out-of-doors. The dining room is at ground level, as in
Alice Millard's house, with the kitchen at one end and two
bedrooms at the other, a level below. Up a winding stairway,
lighted by perforated blocks, is a double-height living room
seemingly carved out of concrete. One textured wall gestures
toward the hearth, while across from it pillars of blocks frame
the window view; terraces open off either side of the room.
Spaces move fluidly from earth to sky, penetrating and
withdrawing in dynamic motion. Each of the four textile-
block houses has its own distinctive block patterns; the
Storer House's eleven designs were woven with plain blocks
to produce rich textures: solid, perforated with glass infill,
lighted, and open to the air. Here Wright's team inserted
horizontal and vertical steel rods ("steel the spider, now
spinning a web") to reinforce each course of hollow blocks.
Rather than use mortar, they poured in concrete grout to
strengthen the seal. And they cast the blocks in metal rather
than wooden molds for more uniformity. It was a novel system
designed to bypass expensive skilled workers and costly
materials—so that the house could almost build itself.

FREEMAN HOUSE

Concrete had fascinated Wright long before he designed the four textile-block houses in Los Angeles in 1923. He liked the monolithic look of this architectural "outcast" and used it in 1905 for the innovative Unity Temple in his hometown of Oak Park. The next year he designed for an Illinois client what he regarded as his first house of concrete blocks (never built). Those blocks, however, lacked the shadow-catching patterns Wright was to draw for his California commissions. His experiments beginning in 1913 with textured stone at Midway Gardens in Chicago and then the Imperial Hotel in Tokyo emboldened him to try richer designs in residential settings. The dominant block motif for the Freeman House in Los Angeles—a modern-day fossil impressed with fallen plants—is perhaps an allusion to trees shading the central cube form. Fifty variations served as multihued threads in the house's warp and woof of twelve thousand blocks. But here glass became an equal part of the composition, with streams of light woven into the solidity of the concrete. Sectioned windows mimic the form of the blocks and then slide around corners to make the walls evaporate. In no time Wright made these mitered-glass corners one of his signatures. Inside, floor-to-ceiling windows on three sides open the living area to incomparable views. In contrast, the fireplace opposite— a necessity for Wright, even in sunny California—offers comforting shelter. Recognizing the coming of more casual lifestyles, the dining room occupies part of the living area. Two bedrooms below have access to a terrace ringed with walls capped in decorative block. Wright's son Lloyd served as on-site supervisor for the California houses, and Rudolph M. Schindler, a former Wright student, helped with projects such as the furnishings for the Freeman House. For both of the young men, working for Wright was often a thankless task.

ENNIS HOUSE

For the most monumental of his concrete-block houses, Wright returned to the pre-Columbian legacy of Hollyhock House. Rising on its ridge in Los Angeles, Charles and Mabel Ennis's 1923 house clearly calls up the primitive "earth-architecture" that inspired Wright even as a boy. Textile-block walls thread themselves sideways into the earth while templelike pavilions push sunward. Just as modern artists in Europe were rejecting traditional Western images, Wright seemed to be seeking something simpler and purer in his architectural palette. The powerful block pattern here—radiating squares holding light and shadow—only enhanced the sculptural effect. From the dark cave in the entry court that serves as the door, stairs lead upward toward the light. Running nearly the length of the house, past the dining room, living room, and bedrooms, straddling two terraces, is an interior loggia that bridges the man-made and natural worlds. It pauses in the living room to rise a half story and announce the hearth, which ascends in a glittering overmantel mosaic of wisteria modeled after ones Wright had used early in his practice. Art glass windows and doors, not seen in the previous textile-block houses, appear uncomfortable if not equally anachronistic in this rough-hewn temple. The owners themselves were responsible for the shiny marble floors and wrought-iron work that had never been part of the architect's vocabulary. Although machine-made, his textile-block houses were meant to be as natural as the mountains—earth houses. Wright had, in fact, mixed in soil from the building site to bind each block organically to the earth (a move that unwittingly hastened their deterioration). Uniform in production but individualized by their signature motifs, they were, claimed Wright, limited only by imagination. Today his unique imprint on the Ennis House has made it a recognizable backdrop in numerous movies and advertisements.

LLOYD JONES HOUSE

Once mastered, concrete remained a staple building material for Wright to the end of his career. "Tough, light, but not 'thin'; imperishable; plastic; no unnecessary lie about it anywhere and yet machine-made, mechanically perfect," he wrote in 1929, the year he stretched this once-despised material to unforeseen beauty. In the Oklahoma home for his cousin Richard Lloyd Jones, founder of the Tulsa *Tribune*, Wright played on the block-and-glass rhythm he began in the Freeman House. But here he pushed the concrete blocks to the background and brought glass to the fore to make Lloyd Jones's Westhope a "dwelling house without walls." Even though larger, at twenty inches wide by fifteen inches high, the blocks recede in importance because they are for the most part unornamented on the exterior. Windows sectioned in steel to mirror the blocks fill the voids between solid piers—Wright called the alternating rows "palisades." Nearly transparent conservatories reach out into the landscape and capture sun for plants inside. Primarily two stories high with stepped-down wings, the house wraps around a courtyard furnished with a garden and pool. The dining room is secluded inside, away from window walls, but it rises to an expansive living room where light prevails. High clerestory windows above simply patterned blocks direct light downward to meet more light coming in on either side. Electric lights are inset into occasional blocks to vary the tempo. Bedrooms and a library are on one side, with more bedrooms above. A covered walkway leads to a garage and servants' quarters. Although the plan recalls the one Wright used for another newspaperman, Henry Allen, here he bypassed the horizontal sense of shelter embodied in his earlier houses built on the prairie. Instead, crystal-thin glass, under a simple flat roof, takes over that role. The momentum has shifted upward, like the Hollywood hills, indicating that the freedom of Wright's "California Romanza" continued to shape his work even after he moved eastward.

FALLINGWATER

Wright no doubt was thankful in later years that he took into his new architectural fellowship in 1934 a young man named Edgar Kaufmann Jr. Wright's *Autobiography*, published in 1932 in part to revive his flagging career, attracted many admirers (more than clients), and Kaufmann was one of them. His parents, Edgar and Liliane Kaufmann, who owned a spot near a waterfall in Pennsylvania where they liked to sunbathe, came to Taliesin to visit their son. The rest is architectural history. In 1935 Wright designed them a country retreat that has become the most famous private house in the world. Fallingwater emerged from his imagination fully formed. It would cantilever over the rocks into nature just like a tree, its branching terraces of reinforced concrete poised daringly right over, not just near, the Kaufmanns' favorite waterfall in Mill Run. A central core of stacked sandstone, inset with windows in autumn-red frames, would rise high to anchor the house to the valley. The hearth would be carved from boulders already in place. It was a tour de force that put Wright on the cover of *Time* in 1938, the year after the house was completed. Fallingwater responded to the "music of the stream," he said, and it plays throughout the house. Broad terraces put the family and guests over the water as if they were standing on a rocky ledge; a hatchway led them down into a natural pool. Glass walls on the three levels frame views of the rocky site and the embracing forest. Up an ingenious covered pathway is a guest house Wright added in 1939. Everywhere the rhododendron color of the concrete terraces against the natural gray stone proclaims the hand of the architect, as do windows butted directly into rough walls. Wright was here, they say, showing the modernists how to design a machine for living in nature. It was a place to listen to "the quiet of the country," interrupted only by the stream's faint melody.

WINGSPREAD

Before the decade of the Great Depression was out, Wright was given the opportunity in 1937 to design another great house for a wealthy patron. Just the year before, Herbert F. Johnson had asked Wright to give his company, the maker of Johnson Wax, a new headquarters. The resulting S. C. Johnson and Son Administration Building and its later Research Tower of 1944 in Racine, Wisconsin, have since become international landmarks. For Johnson's home at nearby Wind Point, Wright produced what he called his last Prairie house, but it was already looking forward. The tiered brick structure is Wright's most pronounced pinwheel, its four arms spinning out from a three-story "wigwam" at the center. Here an elliptical chimney under a tier of octagonal clerestories helps section the space into living, dining, and quiet areas, complete with a mezzanine and spiral stair to the rooftop. Wings zoned for different activities reach out to the sides: one for the children, a raised level holding the master suite with an observation perch, another for guests, and the fourth containing the kitchen and servants' quarters. A swimming pool fills the nook near the children's wing, adjacent to a playroom that angles out to meet it. On the garden side a pergola stretched over columns of delicate metal piping provides shade the length of the wing. Wright anticipated "wild grapevines swinging·pendent from the generously spreading trellises." Except for the red brick they had in common, Johnson's home was as different from his office building as the two men had seemed when they first met. They were "at each other's throats," the grandson of the company founder recalled of his first meeting with his seventy-year-old architect. Wright redeemed himself, as he usually did, in his actions rather than through his words.

TALIESIN WEST

To his already full palette, Wright in the late 1930s added new inspirations: the sere earth tones of desert boulders, the peaks of mountains rising majestically, the natural engineering of the cactus. In 1937 he set up camp in the desert of Scottsdale, Arizona, and painted his new winter retreat, Taliesin West, with shadows cast by the unrelenting sunshine. Like an artist, he was drawn to desert light and color. He first visited Arizona in 1927 and then returned two years later to supervise a resort project that quickly plummeted with the stock market. The cabins he and his associates built in 1929—"like a group of giant butterflies" on desert outcroppings—survived only in memory until he began his southwestern home. Huge boulders were set with sandy concrete in wooden frames to make walls that rose naturally from the site, some sloping inward, others outward. Redwood trusses angled upward as if to thank the McDowell Mountains behind. And overhead translucent canvas roofs made the open pavilions seem to sail through the sandy soil. To *House Beautiful* in December 1946, it was a "luxurious tent." Wright built a drafting room so the Taliesin Fellowship could continue working when it was too cold at Taliesin in Wisconsin. In addition to his own family, Taliesin West accommodated his apprentices and offered entertainment in two theaters. Terraces and courtyards put everyone in touch with nature, while pools and fountains cooled down the desert. For the next twenty-two years Wright and the Fellowship made their annual trek to work in this new environment ruled, said Wright, by the dotted line of strong shadows rather than the straight line of the prairie. During these two decades, between the ages of seventy and ninety-one, it served him as another architectural laboratory. At Taliesin West, noted *House Beautiful*, the ever-youthful archi-tect "has designed not only with stone, wood, and canvas, but has used sun and shadow as if they they, too, were materials."

USONIAN

During his last quarter century Wright enjoyed the work and fame that
seemed to have been denied him in midcareer. But it was not the big
commissions—not even a renowned museum in New York City—that fully
captured his attention. "The house of moderate cost," he wrote in his
1943 *Autobiography*, "is not only America's major architectural problem

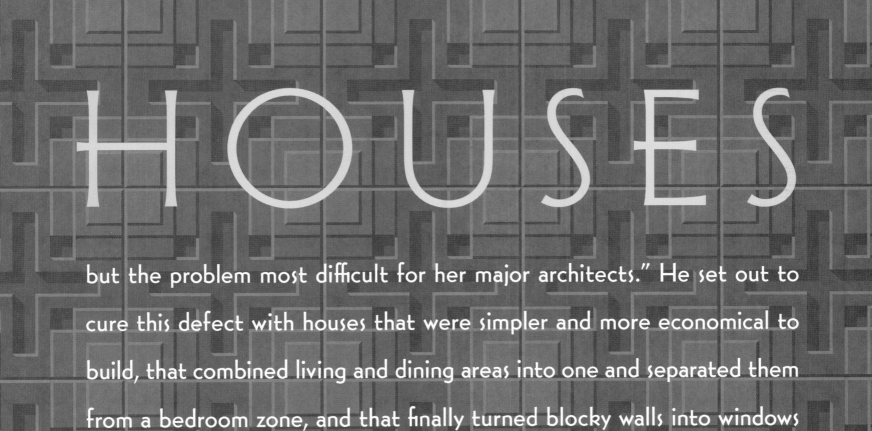

HOUSES

but the problem most difficult for her major architects." He set out to cure this defect with houses that were simpler and more economical to build, that combined living and dining areas into one and separated them from a bedroom zone, and that finally turned blocky walls into windows on nature. Wright's Usonian houses helped change the way we like to live.

FIRST JACOBS HOUSE

Wright never lost his longtime desire to create whole communities based on his principles. To quell modernists who viewed the city as an efficient "machine," Wright in the early 1930s began to flesh out his contrary plan for decentralized suburbs—Broadacre City, he called it. He proposed to take the city to the country and blanket the entire nation with clones of his scheme to house American families on a bucolic acre each. Little came of this grand vision, but Wright began to build Broadacre City house by Usonian house. The first Usonian, designed in 1936, was for Herbert and Katherine Jacobs of Madison, Wisconsin, not far from Wright's Taliesin. For about $5,500—Herbert Jacobs brought in the bricks and did some of the work himself—the family obtained a compact, one-story L-shaped residence of roughly 1,500 square feet. Its streamlined form set the tenor for many of the 140 Usonians that followed: "sandwich" walls faced with pine boards and redwood battens outside and in; supporting brick piers on the exterior and a similar masonry core on the interior; a flat, overhanging roof; a living area private on one side of the house but open to nature on the other through windows and glass doors; the dining nook tucked into the living area across from a small "workspace" kitchen; a back "gallery," or hall, leading to two bedrooms and a study; a red concrete floor holding pipes for gravity heating; and for Wright's favorite machine, the car, a novel "carport" cantilevered seamlessly from the house. This novel residence hugged the ground even tighter than the Prairie houses did. Like all the Usonians, the Jacobs House was built on a geometric module governing horizontal and vertical spaces; here it was a rectangle (inscribed on the floor) of two by four feet wide and thirteen inches high. From standardized materials, economy; from simplicity, a more casual lifestyle for the new American family. Eight years later, the Jacobses signed up for another one.

HANNA HOUSE

Along with so many elements of the traditional house that he had discarded, Wright soon let go of the right angle. Rectangular rooms were no longer sacred—he decided that the obtuse (120-degree) angle was "more suited to human 'to and fro'" and in 1936 pulled a hexagon out of his sleeve for Paul and Jean Hanna's hillside site in Stanford, California. The house slides over the terrain in a large hexagonal plan that embraces dozens of smaller hexagonal modules like a honeycomb. It deserves its nickname: Honeycomb House. As they told *House Beautiful* readers in a January 1963 special issue devoted to their home, the Hannas saw working with Wright as "one of the greatest adventures" of their lives. Their most passionate desire was to be able to change "any detail we wished whenever we wished." Wright's Usonians were tailor-made for change because the nonbearing board-and-batten walls simplified the dismantling process. In 1957 Wright returned to convert the children's bedrooms after they left home, creating a spacious master bedroom suite with a library for the Hannas and opening up the back of the house to match the openness of the front. The playroom became the new dining room. Throughout the living areas, rooms look bigger than they are by visually borrowing space beyond. Changing ceiling heights and floor levels also add subtle variety and dynamism. But an equal part of the house's story is told outside, where it rests on the land like a bee seeking nectar. The house, wrote Curtis Besinger, one of Wright's apprentices, in *House Beautiful,* "is essentially a roof poised lightly above a two-level, paved terrace on the side of the hill." Resembling a hat brim, the roof encircles so many outdoor rooms that the Hannas found they were still discovering new places outside after living there twenty-five years. "The house," noted Besinger, "provides sensations similar to those you might experience within the open, yet protective, shelter of the great oak trees." To the magazine, the Hannas' home was "one of the truly great houses in America."

POPE-LEIGHEY HOUSE

Most of Wright's earliest clients were venturesome business people, members of the new suburban middle class. But in the Great Depression years of the 1930s, his ideas for housing even families on limited budgets appealed to a broader spectrum. "Will you create a house for us? Will you?" Loren Pope, a reporter, wrote to Wright in 1939. *Time* magazine's 1938 story on Wright had introduced him to the architect, and then he borrowed and later bought Wright's 1932 *Autobiography*. They came face to face finally in Washington, D.C., not far from the site in Falls Church, Virginia, where Pope hoped to build a house for his family. In two weeks Wright replied to the written plea: "Of course I am ready to give you a house." In addition to newspapermen, his new generation of clients grew to include numerous teachers. Sided in cypress boards, Pope's one-story L-shaped house reaches out to hold the living-dining area in one arm and the two bedrooms in the other. To the right of the entry is a small "sanctum," or den. Doors along the living area and the dining alcove lead outside. The roof overhangs provide shade, while clerestory windows ring the ceilings to draw in both light and air. Wright's Usonian clients could not afford the art glass that enlivened his Prairie houses, so he gave them an inventive alternative: perforated boards designed to build patterns right into the fabric of the house. The geometric cutout here could be mistaken for a comic turtle but is now thought by one scholar to echo the Hanna House plan. For other houses that followed, different wood patterns hewed an individual personality for each. Wright's Usonians not only were expandable; after it was purchased in 1946 by Marjorie and Robert Leighey, this one also proved that it could be moved. To save it from the path of a highway in 1964, the National Trust for Historic Preservation relocated the house adjacent to its Woodlawn Plantation near Mount Vernon, where it rests today (rebuilt a second time) as a study in contrasting modes of housing. "After having experienced it," Loren Pope told *House Beautiful* readers in August 1948, "no one could ever go back to the painted box, which is all the ordinary house really is, however, elaborate."

87

ROSENBAUM HOUSE

One of the most notable characteristics of Wright's Usonians is that they tend to turn their backs away from the street to secure privacy but open wide on the opposite side to welcome nature. A courtyard embraced by the arms of an L-plan house recalls cloisters of old and gives the interiors the aura of a garden conservatory. Public space and private space—Wright had long taken care to provide for both. The Florence, Alabama, house designed in 1939 for Mildred and Stanley Rosenbaum, a college professor, is one of these proto-typical Usonians. Their three bedrooms, a living-dining area, and a study all leading outside via a terrace grew cramped within less than ten years, however. To Wright, architecture was organic, always changing, so he had foreseen this even-tuality. He viewed his Usonians as evolving "polliwogs," or tadpoles "with a shorter or longer tail." The polliwog's tail depended on the number of children to be housed, and the Rosenbaums had four growing sons. In 1949 their 1,540-square-foot house became the first Usonian to be enlarged, but not by growing a longer tail. Wright instead backed up another L against the original plan, essentially crossing his T opposite the living-dining wing. Here he installed a dormitory and play area and, past a hallway parallel to the original gallery, a guest room and bath tucked into a toelike projection. The addition gave the Rosenbaums a second courtyard, which was later landscaped as a Japanese garden. Wright reflected in 1954 in *The Natural House* that it was important for children to "grow up in building conditions that are harmonious [and] live in an atmosphere that contributes to serenity and well-being."

GOETSCH·WINCKLER
HOUSE

In 1939 Wright was finally handed an opportunity to flesh out his Broadacre City concept in bricks and mortar and trees and grass. Seven Michigan State University professors who had formed a cooperative bought a forty-acre site in East Lansing and asked Wright to design homes for it. Usonia I was to be a self-sufficient community surrounding the educators' own farm fields, which would supplement each home's private garden. But it was not to be: the mortgage financiers denied funding because the plan was unlike anything they were used to. Once again, Wright—clearly disappointed—was ahead of his time. Two of the professors, Alma Goetsch and Katherine Winckler, decided that the chance to have a Wright-designed house was too good to pass up. For the two art teachers the architect devised a compact, 1,350-square-foot home in nearby Okemos that was built in a straight line rather than in an L shape. Poised at the edge of a drop-off, the house is unusually open on both sides but maintains privacy behind screenlike walls of redwood. The entire plan evolved from modules four feet square. Wright let the horizontal pull of the prairie release itself in the one-two-three step of the cantilevered roofs and the streamlined boards. The carport pivots away from the brick chimney serving the main living area, whose brick-walled sitting alcove terminates in a dining table that buffers the view into the kitchen behind it. High but plain clerestories bring in light and views of trees, using glass to ease the transition from wall to ceiling and from inside to outside. Down a short gallery, two bedrooms open onto a terrace. Spaces and views flow as effortlessly here as they do in the three-times larger Hanna House. Only after World War II did one last fragment of Usonia I come to life. In 1949 Erling and Katherine Brauner moved into their new concrete-block home not far from the Goetsch-Winckler House, a design Wright provided to replace the one drawn ten years earlier.

STURGES HOUSE

For Wright, a Usonian was "a thing loving the ground." But faced with a steep building site in the Brentwood Heights district of Los Angeles in 1939, Wright's Usonian ideals soared off the hillside into the sky. At 870 square feet in area, the Sturges House is hardly more than a perfect treehouse. Its living-dining area, two bedrooms, and one bath follow the same in-line plan as the Goetsch-Winckler House. Because it is in California, a lot of living can take place outside. Wright liked "as much vista and garden coming in as we can afford," so he encircled the small house with a balcony that follows the same six-foot, six-inch-square module as the interior. Rustic lapped redwood siding, originally stained a rust color, adds to the sense of being among the trees. Above the balcony a trellis perforated with squares acts like a forest canopy to create shade inside and out; instead of leaves, however, its shadows recall the square module of the plan and reinforce Wright's sense of geometry. The entire house pirouettes over its hill on a brick base housing a workshop. Fresh from dangling Fallingwater over a waterfall, Wright carefully conformed a number of Usonians to similarly sloping ground. The Pew House of 1938 in Shorewood Hills, Wisconsin, the Lewis House of 1939 in Libertyville, Illinois, and the Affleck House of 1940 in Bloomfield Hills, Michigan, like the Sturges House and some of Wright's Prairie houses even earlier, took advantage of tricky sites to capture extraordinary views and offer an elevated sense of privacy. "In an organic architecture," he wrote in the April 1935 *Architectural Record*," the ground itself predetermines all features; the climate modifies them; available means limit them; function shapes them." In Brentwood Heights, the ground dictated a Fallingwater for Everyman.

AULDBRASS PLANTATION

For another of his rare southern commissions, Wright let
the ground speak to him again—but the site of Auldbrass
Plantation in Yemassee, South Carolina, was radically different
terrain, one filled with cypress trees floating out of swamp-
lands and spreading live oaks veiled with Spanish moss.
C. Leigh Stevens's idea in 1939 was to create a modern-day
plantation complete with workers' cottages and outbuildings
from a barn to stables, kennels, chicken runs, and space for
a caretaker. A guest house, lake, and barge to ferry guests
around the estate were never constructed, but the structures
that were built form a land apart that is as cohesive as Taliesin
and Taliesin West. Where deep quarries of stone and tall,
angular mountains, respectively, served as models for his
Wisconsin and Arizona homes, here Wright turned to the trees
for inspiration. In the main house walls of tidewater cypress
lean inward as if they were trunks bent by time. Limbs of
wood dance on the generous windows, tracing branchlike
motifs. Overhead in the living area a canopy of beams crowns
the board-lined ceiling. Two levels of perforated clerestory
windows filter sunlight and stencil patterns on the red
concrete floor, which is inscribed with the house's hexagonal
module. Both the "mansion house" and the two staff cabins (of
seven planned) draw their forms from the hexagon Wright
first used for the Hanna House. Screened porches and, in the
main house, a poolside pergola open the residences to the
out-of-doors. Most of the buildings were linked by esplanades
to reinforce the feeling of being on a southern plantation,
albeit reinterpreted in Wright's fashion. A new owner is
bringing this extraordinary vision back to life, even building
some of the structures and furnishings originally left unfinished.
The breezeway between the living area and the distant
kitchen—removed from the main house, as in antebellum
days—has been glassed in as a dining room. But today copper
rainspouts still drip from copper roofs in abstract versions of
the moss and sinuous vegetation that fed Wright's imagination.

SECOND JACOBS HOUSE

Following his own admonition that no house should ever be on a hill but should be of the hill, Wright designed a second home for his former clients the Jacobses in 1944. His design for their new house in Middleton, Wisconsin, near Madison, brought the hill to the house in the form of an earth berm that snuggles up to the second story like a collar keeping out chill winter winds. On the house's private side is perpetual summer: a concave wall of glass that invites the sun inside. Conceived three decades before America's energy crisis, this passive solar collector was christened by Wright his first "solar hemicycle." Windows atop doors leading outside provide two stories of light and warmth. The sun's heat is absorbed by the roughly laid stone walls and radiated back at night. In the hot months a roof overhang offers shade, while clerestories vent overheated air to the outside. Ranged along the glass wall downstairs is a gently curving forty-foot-long living area terminating in the workspace kitchen. Above are five bed-rooms entered off a balcony set back from the south-facing windows. A stone-lined tunnel through the earth berm deposits residents and guests in the hemicycle, which frames a caldera carved into the prairie to serve as the family garden. A circular pool begins on the terrace but plays a game by completing itself only indoors, in the living area on the other side of the glass; each half circle mimics the shape of the house itself. Two other semicircles punctuate the berm-front walls to house the fireplace and a utility core that rises to the second floor to hold the bathroom. With its two stories adroitly hidden behind a grassy mound, one can hardly tell where the building ends and nature begins. Here Wright succeeded in meeting our competing needs for shelter and liberating space.

CEDAR ROCK

As he had a number of times earlier in his career, Wright in 1945 tested the waters for one of his design ideas by publishing a prototype in the *Ladies' Home Journal*. His plan for a house of glass happened to suit a spectacular site clients brought him, overlooking the Wapsipinicon River in Quasqueton, Iowa. Lowell and Agnes Walter could not move into their retirement home, named Cedar Rock, until 1950 because of a building materials shortage brought on by World War II, but it was worth the wait. Their living room, high on the bluff, gave them a front-row seat on nature. Wright angled the space thirty degrees off the stem of the house to frame views up and down the river. From this glass-walled pilot house, its windows mitered at the corners to make the walls disappear, the Walters could captain their own ship. Open also to the sky by holes pierced in the concrete roof, the living area was in every sense—as Wright called it on the plans—a garden room. A broad front trellis and planters beneath the windows filled the views with greenery, while sunlight streaming through the ceiling coaxed a garden to thrive indoors as well. Freed from the need during the Great Depression to economize with exterior materials such as board and batten, this and later Usonians indulged in more substantial masonry. Here it was brick, whose form and color are replicated at the riverside in a pavilion designed in 1948. Containing a boathouse below and a retreat above, the miniature structure boldly projects itself toward the water in a typically Wrightian gesture of assertion and control. Up on the bluff Wright allowed himself an old-fashioned feature: he built a "council fire" recalling masonry rings Prairie School landscape architects created to add a note of mysticism to their gardens. Encircling seats encouraged people to gather around the fire of an evening and tell stories, enhancing a feeling of togetherness and community.

98

SMITH HOUSE

For another teacher, Melvyn Maxwell Smith, and his wife, Sara, of Bloomfield Hills, Michigan, Wright in 1946 reached back to his Usonian standbys of a decade earlier. He produced a compact L shape with board-and-batten siding of tidewater cypress. At the core of these composite walls was a sheet of plywood covered on both sides by a waterproof membrane; the interior and exterior boards were then attached with battens screwed into the "sandwich." By using the same material inside as out, Wright eliminated the need for plaster and trim—the walls became their own decoration. Cutout screens on the doors and above the dining table further proved wood's power to create integral patterns as distinctive as Wright's art glass of old yet as economical as Wright's new clients required. Melvyn Smith served as contractor for his house to hold down the expenses, a role a number of other clients took on to maintain budgets that their architect tended to cavalierly exceed. Construction of the Usonians was usually supervised on site by either an architectural apprentice sent out from Taliesin or a master craftsman who could read Wright's mind. In this case John deKoven Hill, a Taliesin fellow, helped raise the Smiths' house, as he did Cedar Rock and others in the 1950s. These stand-ins for Wright often acted as go-betweens to insulate clients and architect, helping ameliorate problems that typically arose. After moving into their three-bedroom house in 1950, the Smiths decided in 1969 to enlarge the house via the "polliwog tail," the bedroom zone, calling on Wright's successor firm, Taliesin Associated Architects. One of the last significant Usonians to rely on wood siding, the house presents a classic profile of what Wright was trying to achieve with these designs: a simple and economical yet welcoming home married to the ground.

FRIEDMAN HOUSE

To fulfill the hopes that were sidetracked in 1939 with Usonia I in East Lansing, Michigan, Wright continued trying to build Broadacre City during the 1940s. Three such opportunities came his way in 1947. A group of Upjohn Company employees, also in Michigan, asked him to design a cooperative, the Galesburg Country Homes; after several people splintered off, Wright also laid out plans for Parkwyn Village in nearby Kalamazoo. Each home was to be placed on a one-acre circular lot, but only four Wright houses were built at each. In Pleasantville, New York, he tried again with Usonia Homes. The idea arose with David Henken, who became a Taliesin apprentice to shepherd his idea from dream to reality. Busy with postwar projects, Wright drew up the site plan—one-acre circles that were eventually squared up—but decided that he could not design the fifty-five houses anticipated. Of the three Wright designs to be built, the 1948 house for Sol Friedman, a toymaker, was the first and the most inventive. Perhaps inspired by the client's first name to think of the sun, Wright put him in a circular home of stone that mirrored the round plots he had planned for the community. On the ground floor the living and dining area encircles a stone fireplace in one nearly complete sphere. Abutting this is a semicircle holding the kitchen and a downstairs bedroom. Above, sheltering more bedrooms, the circle is unbroken except for a balcony that visually draws together the two floors. Below, inscribed in the concrete floor, pie slices radiate from the center to underscore the house's round plan. A carport to the left echoes the flying-saucer roof hovering over the house. Masking the house's two-story height, a stone wall unifies the ensemble. By pairing two solar hemicycles to make a complete circle, Wright was able to wrap the house with windows. Here they break out of the rectilinear mode to dip rhythmically into the stone walls with bottoms rounded as if ready to scoop up more light. The Serlin and Reisley families soon joined Friedman in their Wright homes, but Henken and other architects had to build out Wright's scheme. Wright, however, was not yet done with the circles he brought to life in Pleasantville.

WALKER HOUSE

No architect who designed with nature could have hoped
for a site more supremely natural than Della Walker's in
Carmel, California. Beneath gnarled arching pines, the waves
of Monterey Bay crash along a rock-strewn sandy shore.
The rugged view could put the waterfall at Fallingwater
to shame. Wright's answer here was not to tame nature but
to join it. His 1949 design projects a terrace of Carmel stone
onto the coast as if it were the prow of a ship starting out to
sea. The sandy stone echoes the color of the beach, while the
patinated copper roof picks up the ocean's blue-green hues.
"The long white surf lines of the sea," said Wright in 1954,
"seem to join the lines of the house to make a natural melody."
To maximize the vista, he placed the living and dining area
and the kitchen in a glazed hexagon along the shore, leaving
the bedrooms to extend inland in a straight tail toward the
carport. Forming a parallelogram shape overall, the interior
modules divide themselves into four-foot equilateral
triangles—perfect components for building the main hexagon.
Windows, which open downward to minimize gusts, step back
respectfully to the stone walls and are framed in Cherokee
red trim like those at Fallingwater. To Wright the 1,200-square-
foot house was a "cabin on the rocks." If so, it is a ship's cabin,
with its built-in living room sofa compactly tucked under the
windows on three sides to conserve space yet direct views
out to sea. The economy inherent in his Usonian houses,
Wright wrote in the January 1938 *Architectural Forum*,
allowed him "to achieve the sense of spaciousness and vista
we desire in order to liberate the people living in the house."

LAURENT HOUSE

By designing his Usonian houses to fit on one floor, Wright did more than simplify and economize: he made life easier for people such as Kenneth Laurent, a paraplegic whose movement was restricted by a wheelchair. As soon as he learned about Wright's new houses, he knew that one could work for him. The architect agreed to design a home for Laurent and his wife, Phyllis, in Rockford, Illinois, suggesting that a country location would be more soothing. Wright's 1949 plan revived the solar hemicycle concept he had recently built for the Jacobs family but closed the concave arc with an opposing convex terrace. The resulting elliptical plan became one he liked enough to repeat a number of times, including in the house for his son Robert Llewellyn Wright. A terrace, said Wright, should be more than just a path between two points—it should always meet its potential to be an outdoor room. On the Laurent terrace, waves of ellipses create a dynamic room every bit as interesting as those roofed over. Near the window wall a small elliptical pool holds the edge of a larger greenery-filled ellipse, which is ringed by a concrete walkway and a brick wall that complete the house's football shape. Floor-to-ceiling glass doors and windows—"as much a part of the design as eyes are part of the face," said Wright in 1943—scribe a quiet line between outdoors and indoors. Arrayed along this wall of glass is the Laurents' main living area: a long, narrow garden room that follows the hemicycle's arc to close the circle that begins outside with nature.

PALMER HOUSE

Today few teachers and journalists dare to dream of asking an architect of international stature to design a house for them. But in the last two decades of Wright's life, Alma Goetsch, Katherine Winckler, Herbert Jacobs, Loren Pope, Stanley Rosenbaum, and their peers did just that. In 1950 William Palmer, a professor at the University of Michigan in Ann Arbor, and his wife, Mary, a musical theorist, joined them. They respected his ideas, and they shared his love of music. Over a half century, like members of a Wrightian orchestra, they have interpreted the master's composition with precision and added a coda or two of their own. In the Palmers' house the triangle—perhaps not coincidentally also a musical instrument—leads the theme. A triangular terrace, a dining alcove, and a living space (furnished with a grand piano) fill the three points of a large triangle, which segues into another triangle enfolding the workspace kitchen. The master bedroom takes over another, introducing a string of interlocked triangles that hold two more bedrooms and a triangular study, all fleshing out the in-line plan. The house's motif is underscored by triangles scribed in the waxed red concrete floor, whose rosiness blends with tidewater cypress paneling to suffuse the house with autumnal warmth. Triangular tables and hassocks pick up the motif. A strikingly cantilevered carport shows the way to the front door of the one-story house straddling a ridge, where perforated blocks in the brick wall announce the house's plan. At the opposite end, off the living area, terrace steps lead to a Japanese garden designed by the Palmers and a brick teahouse added in 1964 by John Howe. A former Wright apprentice, Howe produced similar expansions for other Wright clients. Mary Palmer was attracted to Wright's work because she saw in it the harmony of a Beethoven quartet. Here Wright, who was taught by his father to regard classical music as an edifice of sound, became Beethoven's equal.

109

ZIMMERMAN HOUSE

In the living room of Isadore and Lucille Zimmerman's 1,458-square-foot home in Manchester, New Hampshire, Wright had to carve out a space not only for his clients' usual grand piano. The couple also wanted a roofed wooden music stand for their chamber music evenings just as he had fashioned for himself at Taliesin. Music became a theme for both architect and clients. Wright created a concert alcove for the Zimmermans at the far end of their living room, where they and their friends could play surrounded by windows. Typical for Usonians, this house has a street side whose privacy is punctured only by a frieze of concrete-trimmed square windows punched in the brick wall—a treatment reprising some of Wright's Prairie houses. The masonry's solidity dissolves on the opposite side in a screen of glass from one end of the house to the other. Beginning in the music corner, four large square windows repeat the square motif of the high windows lining the long, narrow room. Framed in wood like works of art, they are surrounded by glass panels that bring nature into this garden room. French doors lead from the dining nook onto the back terrace. The overhanging gabled roofs, here capped by a clerestory, also call to mind the houses Wright first built on the prairie more than his recent flat-topped Usonians. But the house is in every respect a "companion to the horizon," one showing, as Wright suggested in 1943, "the new sense of space, light and freedom—to which our U.S.A. is entitled."

DAVID WRIGHT HOUSE

From the time he started rearranging boulders to build Taliesin West in 1937, Wright had been exploring how to live in the desert. He wondered, for instance, how the leafy canopies of citrus groves dotting Phoenix might become "the lawn of the house." When his son David Wright asked for a home for himself and his wife, Gladys, in the midst of such a grove, the father in 1950 turned to a prototype called "How to Live in the Southwest." Reached by a path of round stepping stones, a sinuous ramp spirals up from the ground like a desert dust storm—their house in 1953 reminded Pedro E. Guerrero, Wright's photographer, of "a coiled rattlesnake poised to strike." From the shaded garden court with its elliptical pool to the plan itself, circles form the core of this composition. Encircling the elevated living area along the dining alcove, past two bedrooms, and down to a cantilevered master bedroom, a balcony provides fine prospects of mountains and a lawn of citrus trees. Windows, some of them half moons, line the elevated balcony on one side and look into the courtyard on the other. One massive cylinder holding the utilities below and the kitchen above visually anchors the house to the earth, aided by two smaller towers containing a fireplace for the living area and one for the master bedroom. The snaking ramp continues up to a roof garden. "You marvel at the lack of right-angle corners, those traps for the spirit and the vision," said *House Beautiful* in November 1955. Because David Wright promoted the use of concrete block—an interest no doubt inherited from his father—the whole is wrapped in basic concrete block as rugged as the desert. Its plainness is relieved only by a decorative bottom course of cast concrete whose elliptical stamp is the same shape as the house and pool. Like unfurled parasols, the roofs and a vine-covered trellis projected out from the living area provide some relief from the burning desert sun. But despite the refreshing vistas of orange trees afforded by the raised design, Wright's architectural gymnastics put his son up just high enough to catch the heat as it rose off the desert floor. Here Wright had to abandon natural cooling in favor of air conditioning.

R. L. WRIGHT HOUSE

Three years after designing David Wright's desert spiral, his father took the petal-like concrete motif from that house and turned it into a home for his youngest son, Robert Llewellyn Wright (known as Llewellyn). This house in Bethesda, Maryland, designed in 1953, is a true ellipse, convex on both sides. It shows a steady evolution in Wright's manipulation of his compass from the solar hemicycle of the second Jacobs House of 1944 through the Laurent House of 1949, which is completely elliptical only when the terrace is considered. In typical Usonian fashion, the house for Llewellyn Wright, an attorney, and his wife, Elizabeth, is clearly two sided. At the front is mystery and privacy: austere concrete block, as at his brother David's house, relieved chiefly by a frieze of pierced openings lighting the upstairs gallery. At the rear of the densely wooded lot the design turns into a treehouse, its upper walls and cornice covered in Philippine mahogany boards recalling the interior paneling of David's house. With its pointed, prowlike ends and an elliptical balcony cantilevered from one wall, the house seems to sail through the forest. A front tower, an idea also borrowed from David's home, holds the bathroom above the kitchen. Outside this circular workspace, the dining alcove opens into an exceptionally airy almond-shaped living area, whose doors lead to a circular terrace and an elliptical pool poised over a ravine. Upstairs, two bedrooms and the balconied master bedroom rest in freeform spaces carved out of the ellipse. Inside and out, concrete blocks curve with the ease of plastic into graceful walls. Back in 1928 Wright had declaimed in *Architectural Record* that these blocks were the most inferior building material around—"abominable ... downright vicious ... relegated to the backyard of aesthetic oblivion." But he had plans even then for converting this "despised thing" into a "thoroughbred," returning to its mechanical origins to make it "a mere mechanical unit in a quiet, plastic whole." Concrete block was humble, he said, only "before Imagination enters."

TONKENS HOUSE

Rescued by Wright's boundless imagination, even in his late eighties, concrete block remained a favorite building material for the architect until he designed his last house in 1959. Wright had decided in 1949 to once again build whole houses out of reinforced blocks—as he had shown he could do in Los Angeles three decades before. This time the blocks were plain, not textured, and Wright's system was meant to be so simple that the houses could almost build themselves. He called them Usonian Automatics and claimed that they were designed for returning G.I.s on limited budgets: the mason, the carpenter, the plasterer, and their costly fellow union members were all to be eliminated, leaving homeowners merely to find their own sand and put the blocks together themselves. Of the handful of the resulting build-it-yourself homes, a continuing theme in Wright's Usonia, one of the most luxurious is the Tonkens House of 1954 in Amberley Village outside Cincinnati, Ohio. The blocks, two feet wide by one foot high, were made and stacked by a contractor, although other clients did indeed pitch in as Wright suggested. Most of the blocks are open, making them lighter to work with and easy to inset with glass. Walls thus practically vanish in perforated screens inviting in light and air. Concrete inside as well as out, the Tonkens House has a ceiling composed of coffered blocks, some of them leafed in gold over the mahogany-paneled gallery. More wood in built-in bookcases and cabinets and light from clerestories warm up the concrete. In the long in-line plan the living area is at one end and the bedrooms and a study in the quiet zone opposite. Floor-to-ceiling doors open the flat-roofed house to a broad terrace on its private side away from the street. Wright succeeded in taking concrete out of the architectural gutter and opening it to the sky.

HAROLD PRICE SR. HOUSE

Concrete made another appearance in 1954 in one of Wright's most daring residences. Showing the infinite variety of this "obedient servant"—more malleable than stone—Wright built an oasis in Phoenix's Paradise Valley neighborhood as welcoming as any desert shelter. At the startling center of his house for Marylou and Harold Price Sr. (Wright's client for the Price Tower of 1952 in Bartlesville, Oklahoma) is an atrium open on two sides to the desert colors and breezes. The copper-edged roof skips like a mirage over paired sets of four concrete-block piers that pyramid downward. Slender steel pipes that actually carry the weight almost evaporate into insignificance. Inside the open-air room, under a square skylight, are a pyramidal fireplace for cool nights and a round fountain in a square enclosure for hot days. Earth, air, fire, and water—Wright conjured up the four elements in one magical spot. When storms threaten, delightful doors painted by Eugene Masselink, Wright's devoted assistant, can be closed against those same elements. Conceived as a second home where the Prices' grandchildren could stay during vacations, the house soon gained the nickname Grandma House. A virtual dormitory of bedrooms fills the left wing of the house, where a master bedroom was later created from the former children's play area. A swimming pool in front added to the fun of visiting. Located off the atrium in the other direction are the long living and dining area, warmed by a fireplace, and a generous kitchen. Past a loggia, angled forward to embrace the desert, is the guest wing and carport. Every-where, concrete sets the tone—cool and gray, stepped up and down to emphasize its intrinsic blockiness—forming ornament as organic as the spiny cacti populating the desert.

RAYWARD HOUSE

Windows curved to catch the sun, a plan almost daring nature, a quiet zone and an active zone, an ellipse, circles, square modules, rectangular concrete blocks—many of the themes of Wright's productive last years came together in the Rayward House of 1955 in New Canaan, Connecticut. Magnificently nestled into the shoreline of a rock-strewn pond, the house reaches out to nature but with more reticence than Fallingwater. The dining and living area, divided by the kitchen, curves along the site's most picturesque point in a solar hemicycle reminiscent of the second Jacobs House from a decade earlier. Tall windows and doors, divided horizontally near the ceiling to telegraph their height, look onto a terrace that forms the far side of the ellipse. A half level below is a circular pool, and below that lie a dam and waterfall in the pond. The house's name, Tirranna, an aboriginal term translated as "running waters," seems apt. Not as compact as Wright's earlier elliptical designs, the one-story structure breaks out of its pure geometric form to shelter a study, carport, and maid's room to the right and a bedroom wing to the left. In 1958 Wright expanded the bedrooms into an L-shaped zone terminating in a new master bedroom; a glass-domed observatory brought the Raywards even closer to nature. Hiding in an elliptical playhouse added at pondside in 1957, their children could pretend that they were in a cave. That perfect 1950s icon, a personal bomb shelter, occupied the small basement under the carport wing. Concrete for protection, for economy, for sheer virtuosity: Wright knew how to turn it to best advantage. Robert (Byron) Mosher, one of Wright's former apprentices, wrote in the November 1955 *House Beautiful* that "the materials of building are to the creative architect what words are to the poet. But materials, as words, must express their true meaning to be beautiful and real."

LYKES HOUSE

Fittingly, Wright's last house was designed for a cactus-filled
site in Phoenix not far from Taliesin West, his winter home.
Aime and Norman Lykes's property, however, was as steep
as his was flat. In 1959 Wright, then ninety-one years old, had
time to do little more than sketch out his ideas for them
before he died in Phoenix on April 9. Circles were on his mind,
as they had been for nearly a half century. He envisioned two
observation towers that would unite house and view. After
Wright's death John Rattenbury, one of his apprentices, took
over to flesh out the concept, but construction did not begin
until 1966. The house is a joyous poem to the freedom of walls
without corners. On the plan circles collide like the balloons
Wright brought home to his children in the 1890s, as fascinated
as they with the lighter-than-air spheres. A circular entrance
court leads to a circular garden court, where a pool has since
been added, and then into the smaller protected sphere of
the living and dining area. Across from the circular fireplace
a run of windows offers a panoramic view of Phoenix as
well as, from glass doors, the front terrace and courtyard. Up
a spiral stairway a hideaway office has an even higher prospect.
On the main level a back gallery leads past the bedrooms to
the master bedroom occupying the second tower, a slightly
smaller circle that acts as an exclamation point to the
inventive plan. Even the kitchen adopts the circular motif,
complete with half-moon windows to suitably frame the view.
True to Wright's twenty-five-year odyssey in search of an
economical yet rich way to build, the house relies on concrete
block's versatility to turn its sleek corners. Five years before
dashing off this last idea, Wright had reasserted in *The
Natural House* that moderate-cost houses were America's
most pressing architectural problem. "As for me," he wrote,
"I would rather solve it with satisfaction to myself and Usonia,
than build [almost] anything I can think of at the moment...."

SELECTED BIBLIOGRAPHY

Dunham, Judith. *Details of Frank Lloyd Wright: The California Work, 1909–1974.* San Francisco: Chronicle Books, 1994.

Gebhard, David. *Romanza: The California Architecture of Frank Lloyd Wright.* San Francisco: Chronicle Books, 1988.

Guerrero, Pedro E. *Picturing Wright: An Album from Frank Lloyd Wright's Photographer.* San Francisco: Pomegranate, 1994.

Harrington, Elaine. *Frank Lloyd Wright Home and Studio, Oak Park.* Stuttgart: Edition Axel Menges, 1996.

Hoffmann, Donald. *Frank Lloyd Wright's Dana House.* New York: Dover, 1996.

———. *Frank Lloyd Wright's Hollyhock House.* New York: Dover, 1992.

———. *Frank Lloyd Wright's Robie House.* New York: Dover, 1984.

Levine, Neil. *The Architecture of Frank Lloyd Wright.* Princeton: Princeton University Press, 1996.

Lind, Carla. *The Lost Buildings of Frank Lloyd Wright: Vanished Masterpieces.* London: Thames & Hudson, 1996.

———. *Wright at a Glance Series.* 12 vols. San Francisco: Pomegranate, 1994–96.

———. *The Wright Style.* London: Thames & Hudson, 1992.

McCarter, Robert. *Frank Lloyd Wright.* London: Phaidon Press, 1997.

McCarter, Robert, ed. *Frank Lloyd Wright: A Primer on Architectural Principles.* New York: Princeton Architectural Press, 1991.

Morton, Terry B., ed. *The Pope-Leighey House.* Washington, D.C.: National Trust for Historic Preservation, 1969.

Pfeiffer, Bruce Brooks. *Frank Lloyd Wright: Master Builder.* London: Thames & Hudson, 1997.

Riley, Terence, ed., with Peter Reed. *Frank Lloyd Wright: Architect.* New York: Museum of Modern Art, 1994.

Secrest, Meryle. *Frank Lloyd Wright.* New York: Knopf, 1992.

Sergeant, John. *Frank Lloyd Wright's Usonian Houses: The Case for Organic Architecture.* New York: Whitney Library of Design, 1976.

Storrer, William Allin. *The Frank Lloyd Wright Companion.* Chicago: University of Chicago Press, 1993.

Wright, Frank Lloyd. *Frank Lloyd Wright: Collected Writings.* 5 vols. Edited by Bruce Brooks Pfeiffer. New York: Rizzoli, 1992–95.

PHOTOGRAPH CREDITS

128

INDEX

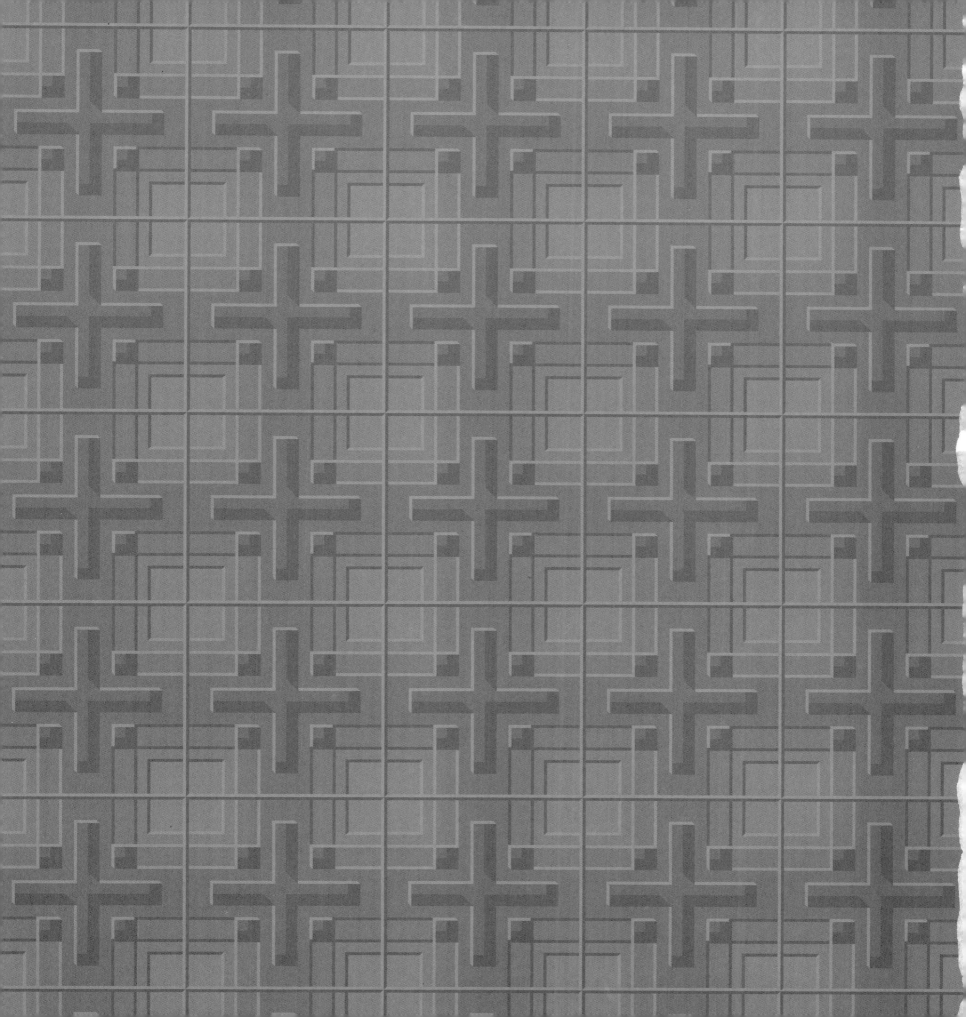

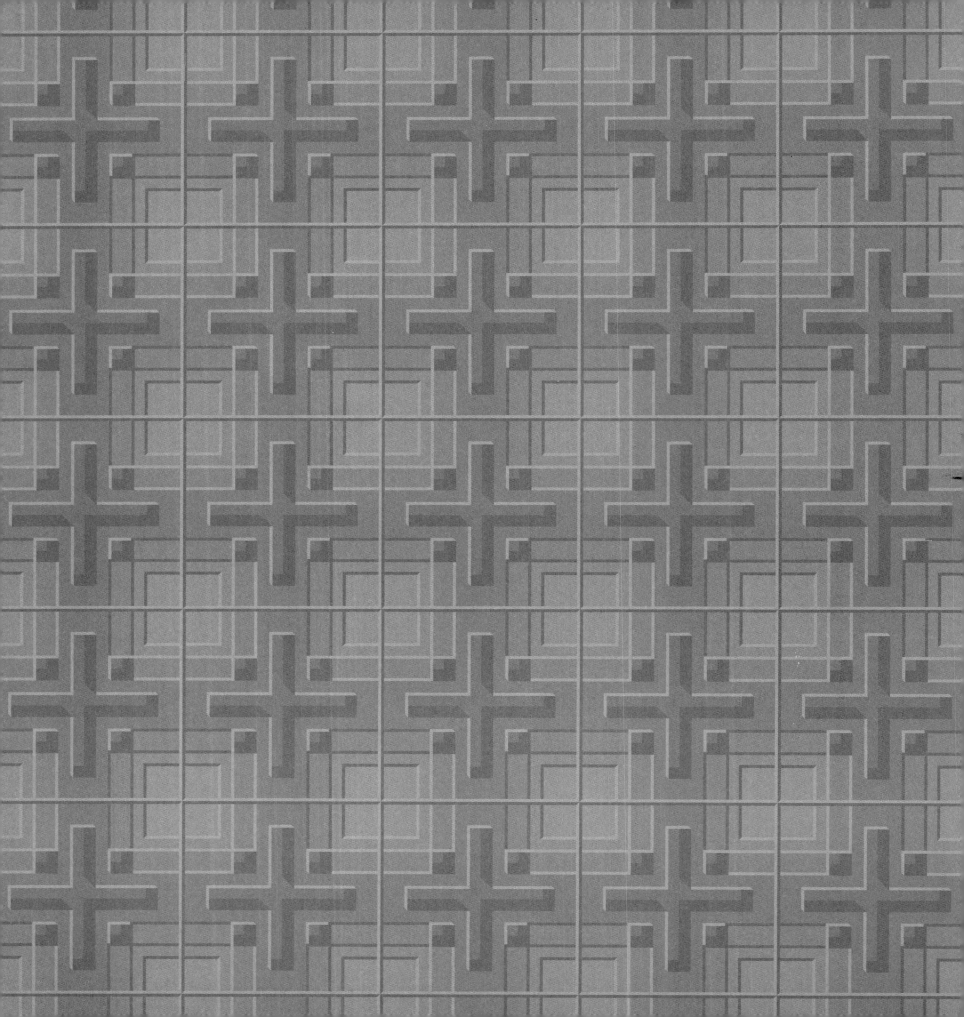